An Introduction
to RhoMobile

Mobile Application Development for Enterprise Data

Matthew Travis

K. Lee Watson

OAK TREE SYSTEMS, INCORPORATED
694 FRONT STREET • LOVINGSTON, VA 22949

Published by Oak Tree Systems, Incorporated

694 Front Street, Lovingston, VA 22949

434.263.6700

http://www.trainingforce.com

http://www.oaktree-systems.com

Date of First Publication: October 2012

ISBN-13: 978-1479275496

ISBN-10: 1479275492

Oak Tree Systems recognizes the trademark information of companies and products within this work, and recognizes those marks with the appropriate use of capitalization.

Oak Tree Systems has made a significant effort to ensure accuracy and completeness of the information provided in this publication. Software development is a rapidly-changing field of study; therefore neither Oak Tree Systems nor the authors can guarantee the information provided will remain accurate.   The procedures and methods shown in this publication are based on the most current information available at the time of publication. This publication is sold and provided without warranty, express or implied. Oak Tree Systems and the authors make no guarantee as to, and assume no responsibility for, the correctness or applicability of the information contained within.

Downloads

Downloads to support this text can be found at Oak Tree's RhoMobile Dropbox site.
URL: https://www.dropbox.com/sh/yuoo3jb5k5qk9ah/rIuM6T32U-

Available files include images, along with the completed Rhodes and RhoConnect application files.

Suggestions, Errata, and Questions

Oak Tree Systems welcomes any feedback readers may have, including suggestions or errata. Please submit all comments to questions@oaktree-systems.com .

About the Authors

Matthew Travis

Matt Travis, a native of Afton, Virginia is a graduate of Virginia Tech. Matt has been working in programming and other related roles at Oak Tree Systems since 1999. Matt gained knowledge of RhoMobile while developing mobile applications for *TrainingForce*, Oak Tree's signature product. During creation of the initial mobile applications, he built additional tools to assist in the development and testing processes. Matt's contributions to this book make developing for the Windows environment less challenging for other developers.

K. Lee Watson

Lee Watson, a graduate of the Jefferson College of Health Sciences and also a former Virginia Tech student, is a training and development specialist. Over a diverse career, Lee has developed e-learning material using a variety of software platforms. He coauthored *MedEMT: A Learning System for Prehospital Care,* significant as one of the first non-computing texts accompanied by an interactive, Flash-based CD-ROM. Although a novice application developer, Lee was able to develop a fully functional instructor application to support *TrainingForce* using RhoMobile. His experiences learning the RhoMobile platform was a major factor leading to the development of this book.

Table of Contents

Introduction

The field of mobile application development is rapidly changing. As the number of available platforms and operating systems continue to grow, application design gets increasingly complex. Designing applications for a single device is largely impractical, even within a single organization. Designing an application once, then building and deploying across multiple devices and operating systems is referred to as cross-platform development. There are a number of software development tools being marketed specifically for that purpose. The challenge for developers is, simply, that most of these platforms are geared towards producing consumer applications. Development of cross-platform mobile applications that allow end-users to efficiently use and update enterprise data is the primary function of Motorola Solutions' *RhoMobile Suite™*.

In late 2011, Oak Tree Systems began looking at cross-platform mobile development tools to support the needs of customers using *TrainingForce*. TrainingForce is a web-based software product for managing training within an organization. The concept was simple – provide a mobile application that extends key functions and integrates technology from a user's device based on their role within the training center. Synchronization of data between the device's local store and the enterprise server was necessary in case an internet connection was not available. After an exhaustive evaluation of products, Oak Tree selected RhoMobile as our development platform.

Important Note: This text is designed to provide general insight for a novice-to-intermediate developer looking to utilize Motorola Solutions' RhoMobile Suite. Coding does not necessarily represent best practices needed for a production application.

Outcomes

An Introduction to RhoMobile has three basic goals. After working through this book, the developer will:

1. Understand the role of Motorola Solutions' RhoMobile in mobile application development.
2. Create a basic Rhodes mobile application.
3. Connect the Rhodes mobile application to a back-end data source using RhoConnect.

Getting Started

Mobile Application or Web Site?

There are significant differences between a mobile application and a mobile web site. Determining the best option for a business need is based on several factors.

A mobile web site requires the device to have and maintain an active network connection. Although mobile data coverage has improved dramatically, there are still many enterprise environments where active connections are impractical or nonexistent. A mobile web site can only store a limited amount of data on mobile devices. Using a mobile web site can also mean some of a device's native features may not be available. For example, a user may not be able to take a photo or video with the device camera and store it remotely. A mobile web site uses the device's browser, increasing usability across a variety of operating systems and device sizes.

Some developers take a hybrid approach to balancing between mobile applications and sites. Some mobile applications function as a "wrapper" for an organization's mobile web site. These mobile applications use minimal device resources while giving the user quick access to a specific mobile site, often automating the login process and accessing information of specific interest to the end user.

A true mobile application is different in two key ways. First, the applications allow the developer to take advantage of the device's native functions. Today's devices include calendars (personal information managers), contact directories, cameras, GPS devices, and multiple e-mail accounts. Second, the applications may use more of the device's memory and store more data on the device.

Developing an enterprise mobile application can be useful when:

- An individual user needs to access enterprise data in a non-traditional environment, where breaking out a laptop is impractical, or returning to an office is inefficient.
- The user needs to manipulate existing enterprise data rather than enter information.
- The user needs to capture information related to something occurring spontaneously. For example, recording the GPS location and taking photos of an accident scene.
- The enterprise needs to retain ownership of data while allowing the user to access and manipulate it.

The RhoMobile Suite

The RhoMobile Suite is comprised of three distinct products. *RhoStudio* is Motorola Solutions' plug-in for the Eclipse Interactive Development Environment (IDE). *RhoConnect* manages the connection between a deployed application and the enterprise data source. *RhoElements* extends the powerful Rhodes language with additional application programming interfaces (API's) for specific business features such as bar-code reading and signature capture.

A number of cross-platform development tools are currently available on the market. These tools are important because they allow developers to write code once, and then build applications for multiple mobile platforms in a few steps. The ability to reuse code and a common set of API's give development tools great value. A large number of these development tools focus on the creation of consumer applications, incorporating social media and other non-enterprise elements. The number of tools capable of managing the enterprise data needs of an organization is much smaller, and RhoMobile stands out as a leader.

Oak Tree Systems selected RhoMobile as a development platform based on three key factors:

1. The use of a model-view-controller architecture, which was familiar to the development team;
2. The platform's ability to manage data flowing between the enterprise server and user devices; and
3. The ability to deprovision corporate data automatically from an end-user's mobile device, using existing functions.

With continued growth in the employee use of personal devices in the workplace, the ability to deprovision those devices is extremely important. When an employee resigns or is terminated, deprovisioning prevents that employee from corrupting or viewing enterprise data.

RhoStudio

RhoStudio allows development of a single application that is not dependent upon the mobile device's operating system (OS-agnostic). Eclipse is a multi-language software development environment, written primarily in Java, that is free and open-source. RhoStudio installs the Eclipse IDE prepackaged with Motorola Solutions' RhoStudio plug-in, allowing easy installation of the platform and rapid development of Rhodes and RhoConnect applications.

RhoStudio is used to develop both the Rhodes application for deployment to the end-user device, and the RhoConnect application that provides data to the mobile device. When a Rhodes application is used in conjunction with RhoConnect, data is served up according to the application's rules. A software-based simulator allows rapid prototyping; the simulator interacts with the data sources in the same manner as an actual mobile device.

In addition to gaining familiarity with the Eclipse IDE and RhoStudio plug-in, developers should also gain familiarity with Rhodes (the Ruby-based development framework), GEMS, and JQuery Mobile.

Rhodes & Ruby

The basic application framework for RhoMobile application development is Rhodes, an open source framework based on Ruby. Rhodes is unique among other mobile development platforms because it utilizes Model-View-Controller (MVC) architecture. MVC architecture makes it easy to understand, reuse, and maintain code.
For more information on Rhodes: http://docs.rhomobile.com/rhodes/introduction
For more information on Ruby: http://www.ruby-lang.org/en/

Ruby GEMS

Ruby GEMS are packages containing the necessary code to extend the Ruby framework. GEM versions are very specific. GEMS used by developers must match versions used on production servers; likewise developers working on a shared project should use matching GEM versions.
For more information: http://www.rubygems.info
For more information: http://techiverous.com/2011/05/the-no-nonsense-guide-to-managing-gem-versions/

JQUERY Mobile

JQuery mobile is a framework for creating the mobile application's user interface. JQuery Mobile provides developers with a robust tool set for creating listviews, toolbars, buttons and dialogs.
For more information: http://www.jquerymobile.com

RhoElements

RhoElements represents an extension of the Rhodes programming language. The use of RhoElements is not required to use RhoStudio or deploy applications. RhoElements does provide a number of valuable enhancements for commercial applications.

RhoElements allows the inclusion of HTML device tags and provides access to native Javascript Device API's. Other extensions allow the developer to use near-field communications (NFC), radio-frequency identification (RFID), barcoding, and signature capture API's. RhoElements also allows an application to be built in a "shared mode" which allows multiple applications to access common libraries stored on the device. This eliminates redundant code and conserves device resources.

RhoElements requires additional licensing through Motorola Solutions. To develop with the standard tool set, deselect the "Use RhoElements" box (see Module 1, Exercise 1, Page 10).

RhoConnect

Maintaining the data connection with an enterprise source is a key part of developing a business-oriented mobile application. RhoConnect manages connections to your enterprise data sources. Using RhoConnect, a single application can connect to multiple data sources easily.

The principal function of RhoConnect is to serve up data to mobile devices. Data remains available to users even when the device does not have a network connection. After an initial synchronization, a defined polling interval pushes changed data between the device and enterprise source. By pushing only changed data, performance of the device, the wireless network, and server is maintained. Limiting the data push also respects the mobile carrier's data limits and potential data cost; many mobile carriers imposing a surcharge for high bandwidth or large volume usage.

To support development and administration of applications, RhoConnect also provides an Administration Web Console. The Console provides a wealth of information on the current data available from the enterprise source, as well as details on users and devices.

RhoConnect, as with RhoElements, requires additional licensing. Developers can use a RhoConnect installation on up to 10 devices for application development and testing purposes.

RhoHub & RhoGallery

RhoHub and RhoGallery are web-based development tools that support deployment of RhoMobile applications. While developers are not required to use these tools, for some organizations they are an alternative for building production versions of applications. RhoHub allows a developer to create the application locally in RhoStudio, then build for each platform (iOS, Android, Blackberry, etc.) without having to worry about locally installed software development kits (SDK's). RhoGallery is best described as a private "application store" for each organization that automates application provisioning and deprovisioning.

Note: If developing for Apple's iOS platform, each developer will still need to register with Apple's iOS Developer program (http://developer.apple.com). Apple also maintains an Enterprise Program, designed for organizations that want to develop and deploy applications in-house (without going through the Apple App Store).

RhoHub uses GitHub (http://www.github.com) for migrating code between RhoStudio and RhoHub. GitHub offers numerous options for maintaining control of code revisions and access to repositories.

RhoHub also allows for automated deployment of a RhoConnect application using the Heroku platform. Once a RhoConnect application is migrated to RhoHub, it can be deployed easily.

RhoHub and RhoGallery usage is limited unless a plan is purchased from Motorola Solutions. Many enterprise developers may have concerns or corporate restrictions that prevent hosting data in a public repository such as GitHub or on a public server such as Heroku. Therefore, this book focuses on developing and deploying an application on an internal corporate server.

Basic Concepts

Both novice and experienced developers will find the RhoMobile platform relatively easy to learn and use. The model-view-controller architecture makes the application's structure easy to understand. When a developer begins a new project, RhoStudio generates much of the basic application structure using wizards.

RhoMobile Applications

When a new RhoMobile application is created, the Wizard generates the following folders and file set:

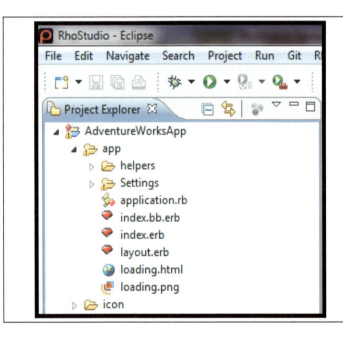

The **\app** directory contains the Models, Views, and Controllers. Code files are designated by the *.rb extension. Extended files for the various views are denoted by the *.erb extension.

Note that the **\app\helpers** directory contains both application and browser helper code files that are available throughout the application.

The **\icon** directory contains the icons used by the mobile device.

The **\public** directory contains images, style sheets, etc.

The **Build.yml** and **rhoconfig.txt** files provide valuable data for the production build of the application.

Once the application is created, a second Wizard allows the developer to rapidly generate models, complete with the associated controller and a number of predefined views.

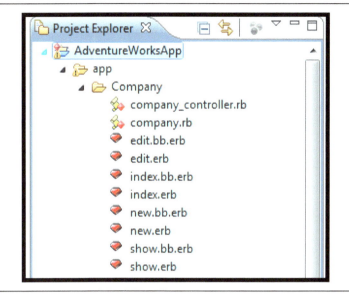

The **<model>.rb** file establishes the Model class. The file determines whether the Model is included in synchronization and provides a location for model-specific code.

The **<model>_controller.rb** file stores methods to manipulate data and set up actions for the view. Create a method for each new action. Wizard-generated controller files contain default actions: index, new, create, edit, update, show, and delete.

The remaining ***.erb** files are views of the data. Each view corresponds to an action within the controller. ***.bb.erb** files are unique to Blackberry devices. These files can contain any valid HTML, JavaScript, or Ruby code. Ruby code is defined using **<%** and **%>** code tags.

Each generated file contains certain basic code elements as a starting point. Generally, each **.erb** file contains the page div, a header div, a content div, and a footer div. These code elements can be modified or deleted as necessary for the finished application.

- Index.erb and index.bb.erb contain code for a listview of items that when selected transition to the show.erb for the individual item. **[Home]** and **[New]** buttons are generated.
- Show.erb and show.bb.rb contain the details for an index list item, along with an **[Edit]** and **[Index]** buttons.
- Edit.erb and edit.bb.rb are form-based views supporting the editing of an index list item. **[Cancel]** and **[Delete]** buttons are generated automatically.
- New.erb and new.bb.erb are a form-based views allowing the user to enter information on a new index list item. A **[Cancel]** button is generated automatically.

Note: One of the challenges associated with RhoStudio is that at least one attribute is required to make use of the Wizard. A workaround is to use a single temporary attribute to generate the model, replacing the temporary attribute as the application is developed. This minimizes the amount of time spent deleting or rewriting code.

Note: Use specific names for models whenever possible. Built-in Ruby class names such as helpers, test, settings, etc. may not be used as model names.

In the individual controller file, Rhodes provides specific methods by default:

- **Index** lists all objects returned using the index.erb view.
- **New** displays a form for creating a new object using the new.erb view.
- **Create** is the method used to create new objects using the information on the form.
- **Edit** displays the parameters of an existing object using an editable form using the edit.erb view.
- **Update** is used to propogate any changed attributes to the database.
- **Show** is the method used to drill down from the index view to an individual object, displayed on show.erb.
- **Delete** is used to delete the entire object.

The Rhoconfig.txt File

The Rhoconfig.txt file is a critical component of the application. A number of parameters are set, including the start page for the finished application. Each parameter is accompanied by a comment line explaining possible settings.

The Build.yml File

The Build.yml file contains additional information for the application. When opened, a "Rhobuild setting" helper tab is displayed. Click **[Add]** to open a window allowing developers to quickly specify phone capabilities used in the application.

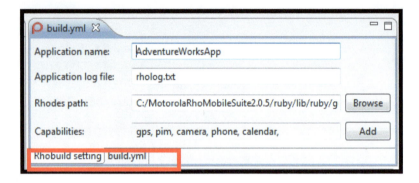

Developers can switch between the "Rhobuild setting" helper and the verbose contents of the build.yml file using the tabs at the bottom of the window.

RhoConnect Applications

Developers can create a RhoConnect application to serve the enterprise data to the Rhodes application. The following file set is created by the RhoConnect Wizard.

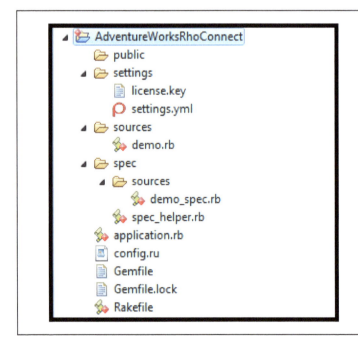

License.Key contains the license information. By default, the included license allows for up to 10 devices.

Settings.yml sets up the server locations and polling intervals for how often RhoConnect will respond to requests for information.

The **Sources** folder contains the source adapter code for each data source.

The **Spec\Sources** folder contains code for the test specifications for each source adapter.

The **config.ru** file contains the parameters for loading the RhoConnect application.

The **application.rb** file contains methods for use throughout the application, such as authentication.

Any time a file in the RhoConnect application is changed, the RhoConnect and Redis instances must be stopped and restarted. *Appendix A* contains the text for a RhoMobile Developer batch file, written to aid developers in working with RhoConnect.

Your Data Source

There are a number of ways to establish a connection between RhoConnect and the enterprise data source. Many enterprise data sources utilize *web services* to exchange information between applications. For example, an inventory management system may use a shipping agent's web service to submit package information. The application built in this text connects to a sample database established on Oak Tree System's server using web services. Web services allow the use of RhoConnect Source Adapters, as well as direct data access through the mobile application. Remember that web service calls made directly from the device will not be available if the device does not have network data access.

Web services are not the only way to connect the application to a data source. There are RhoConnect plug-ins available for Java, Ruby, and .NET. These automate data flow; data operations can be written directly into the enterprise application. Creating RhoConnect plug-ins eliminates the need to create source adapters in the RhoConnect application.

Each enterprise application has different configuration and security needs. Installing a RhoConnect plug-in may be useful for many simple operations, while a source adapter may be more appropriate for combining data from multiple sources.

First Steps

Prior to installing RhoMobile Suite, ensure that Java Development Kit 1.6.0 (JDK) is installed. Also be sure the PATH variable is set to the Java Development Kit in the System Environment. Make a note of the location of the JDK; once the RhoMobile Suite is installed the path to the JDK will need to be specified in *Preferences.*

Motorola Solutions provides the RhoMobile Suite as a single download package available from http://www.motorola.com/Business/US-EN/RhoMobile%20Suite/Downloads. The installation tutorial and notes are located at http://docs.rhomobile.com/rhostudio.tutorial. See Appendix A, *Developer Installation,* page 91.

Writing Code

Rhodes is an efficient coding framework, with a number of elements that aid both novice and experienced developers. The included wizards handle creation of basic application structures. From that starting point, even novice developers can build an effective application.

The URL_FOR Helper Method

The *url_for* application helper method is integral to Rhodes because it abstractly handles the controller navigation within the application. *Url_for* creates links that allow movement across the application structure, passing parameters as well. Although the use of parentheses is not required, they are recommended. *Url_for* can pass additional parameters to the new controller using :query.

Examples

```
# Used to call the :index action and subsequent page within the same model
url_for(:action => :index)

# Used to call the index action and subsequent page from a different model and controller
url_for(:controller => :customer, :action => :index)

# Used to call the options action from the location controller, note the parameters passed using :query.
url_for(:controller => :Location, :action => :options, :query => {:id => @customers.location, :key =>
@params["key"]})
```

Helper Methods

There are a number of helper methods available to the application in the **AdventureWorksApp/app/helpers** directory. The methods are available throughout the application. Methods found in these files are not required. Developers can add, modify, or delete methods as needed. For example, in Module 3 a helper method will be added to determine if a value is blank.

Module 1
Background

Module 1 creates a basic mobile application for an end-user device. This application serves as the foundation for subsequent Modules. These modules work to build a mobile application to accompany a modified Microsoft AdventureWorks sample database. There are four specific exercises in this Module:

- Create the Application Framework
- Create the Company Model
- Edit the Views
- Make it Functional

In order to complete this Module, RhoMobile Suite must be installed in a working configuration.

Outcome

Create a simple mobile application with RhoMobile Suite.

Exercise 1: Create the Application Framework

In this Exercise, the mobile application's base structure is created using a wizard.

1. Start RhoMobile Suite, if not already running.

    a. Go to the "File" menu.
    b. Select "New", "Project". The New Project wizard starts.
    c. From the list of New Project Wizards, open the RhoMobile Folder. Highlight "RhoMobile Application"
    d. Select **[NEXT]**

e. Enter the project name. For this Module, use **AdventureWorksApp**.
    Uncheck the "Use RhoElements" item for this application.
    The "Create application in default workspace should be checked.

f. Select **[Finish]**

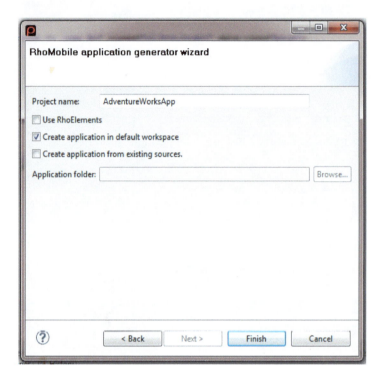

g. The Wizard will display a progress bar and generate the requested application.

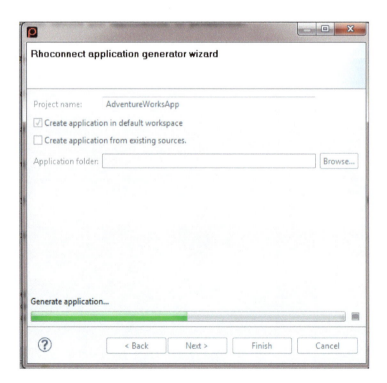

h. The new application will appear in the RhoStudio Project Explorer.

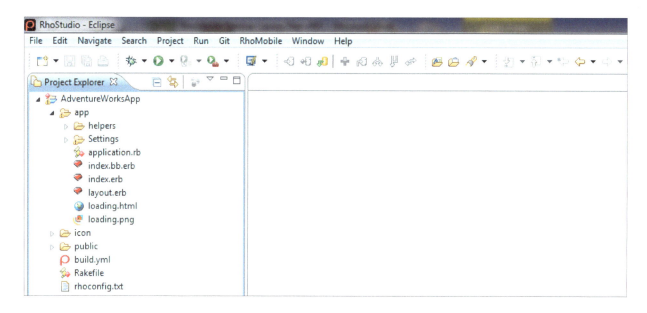

i. Take a moment to explore the resulting application structure.

Exercise 2: Create the Company Model

Now that the basic framework for the mobile application has been established, a model for the Company information is created using the RhoMobile Model Wizard.

1. Right-click on the Project name ('**AdventureWorksApp**').
2. Select "New", "RhoMobile Model"

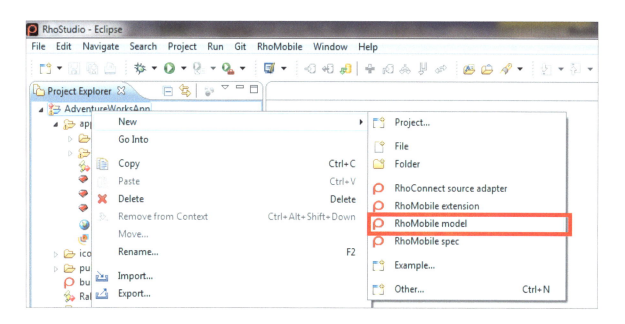

3. The Model Wizard starts and a Model Information screen appears.
   Enter "Company" as the Model name. **Notice the warning**: ⊗ In order for the model to be created using the Model Wizard, at least one attribute must be specified.

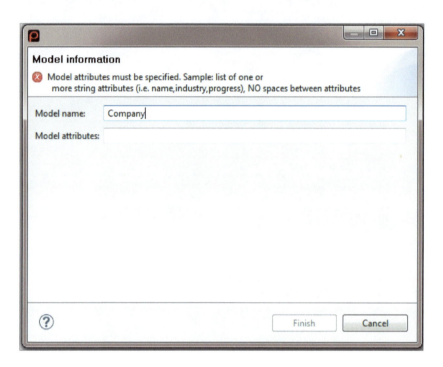

4. Because at least one attribute must be specified, type "a" in the "Model attributes" field and select **[Finish]**. The actual data fields will be edited and specified later.

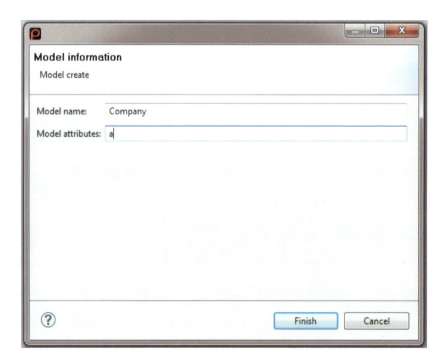

5. The AdventureWorksApp Project is updated and the Company model is visible in Project Explorer in the "App" folder.

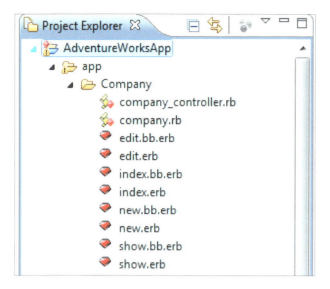

6. Because the Company model will only be used to display information about the AdventureWorks Company, a large number of files can be eliminated. The Model's code file, controller file, and index view are all that are necessary.
    a. Right-click and select "Delete" for each file. Select multiple files by holding down the **[CTRL]** key and left-clicking each file; once all files are selected right-click and select "Delete."
    b. This demo application is being developed specifically for the Android or iOS platform, so all the ".bb" files (BlackBerry platform files) can be deleted.
    c. The edit.erb, new.erb and show.erb files can also be deleted; the index.erb view will display information to the user.
    d. The streamlined Model should look like:

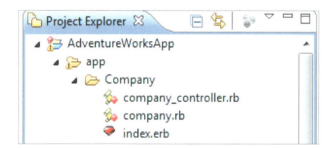

Exercise 3: Edit the Views

The Wizards in Exercises 1 and 2 provide the basic code needed for the application. For example, the **company_controller.rb** file provides basic record create, read, update and delete (CRUD) functions. When looking at the code, here are four things to keep in mind:

- RhoMobile Suite automatically completes many actions, including *"ends", quotation marks, brackets, curly braces, etc.* Be sure to proofread your code. See page 87 for details on how to configure these.
- The Eclipse IDE makes extensive use of highlighting syntax within your code. This can be especially useful at identifying open tags. The colors and options can be changed in the Window, Preferences dialog box. (Ruby, Editor, Syntax Coloring)
- Rhodes modifies capitalization in generating files as necessary using the "_" character. For example, a Model named CourseClass would have a Controller named course_class_controller.rb.
- Use the singular form of names whenever possible. When creating a Model, Rhodes automatically pluralizes the variable on the index function and page, as it assumes they return multiple objects. For example, for a Model "Clients" the variable returns as "@clientses" in the clients_controller.erb and index.erb files.

1. RhoMobile includes a number of base images as part of the Project Creation Wizard, but a number of additional images are necessary to create a functional application. For Android design guidelines, visit http://developer.android.com/design/index.html.

   a. Right-click on the **\public\images** folder, and select "New", "Folder".

---

b. The New Folder Wizard starts.

Ensure the Parent Folder is **AdventureWorksApp\public\images**. The parent folder can be changed if necessary. Enter "Custom" for the folder name. Select **[Finish]**.

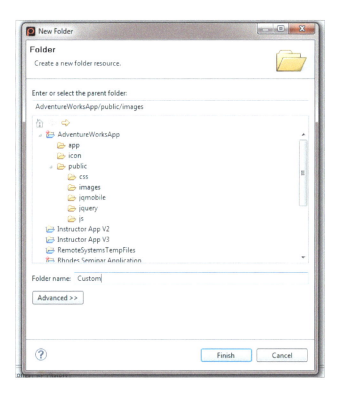

c. Once the Custom folder is created, import the Android Icons. Navigate to Oak Tree's RhoMobile Dropbox site and open the "Android Icons" folder. From the upper-right corner, select "download as a .zip" and save to your computer. Extract the contents of the file to a folder.

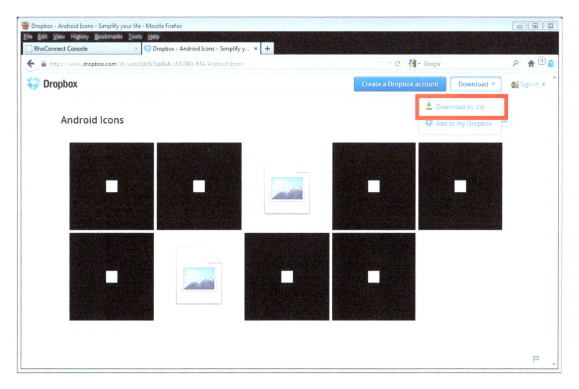

d. Right-click on the Custom folder, and select "Import".

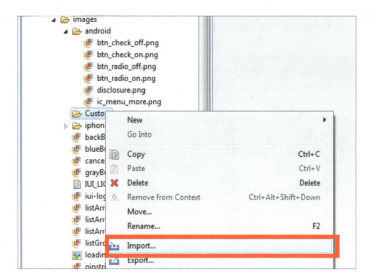

e. The Import Wizard starts.
Select "General", "File System" as the import source and click **[Next]**.

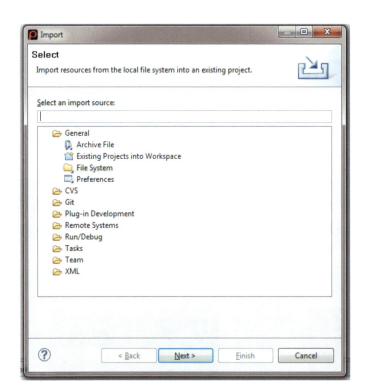

f. The Import Screen opens. Navigate to the directory holding the downloaded files using the **[Browse…]** button. Select individual files or use **[Select All]**. For this application, import the entire library. Once the desired files are selected, click **[Finish]**.

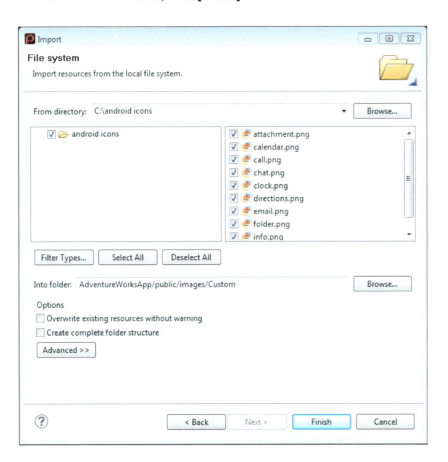

2. Update the Code.
    a. Update the Company Model's **Index.erb** page.
        i. Open **AdventureWorksApp\app\Company\index.erb** by double-clicking it in File Explorer.
        ii. Write the code for the **Index.erb** page.
            1. Note that each page is wrapped in a "page" div, with separate, easily identified divs for the header, content, and footer.
            2. Depending on application design, the developer may want the footer div to float (i.e., immediately follow the content) or be fixed. The footer can be locked to position using `data-position="fixed"`. In this code, the footer contains buttons allowing the device user to contact the Company.
            3. The buttons for the footer are JQuery Mobile. The `data-role="controlgroup"`, `data-mini="true"`, and `data-type="horizontal"` specify how the buttons are grouped on the page.

```
1    <div data-role="page">
2      <div data-role="header" data-position="inline">
3        <h1>AdventureWorks</h1>
4          <a href="<%= Rho::RhoConfig.start_path %>" class="ui-btn-left" data-icon="home" data-
direction="reverse" <%= "data-ajax='false'" if is_bb6 %>>
5            Home </a>
6      </div>
7      <div data-role="content">
8        <div>
9         <h1>AdventureWorks</h1>
10           694 Front Street<br/>
11           Lovingston, VA 22949
12        </div>
13        <div style="text-align: center;">
14          <br/>
15  <img src="http://maps.googleapis.com/maps/api/staticmap?center=694%20Front%20Street%2022949&zoom=15&size=90x1
20&scale=2&maptype=roadmap&markers=size:tiny%7Ccolor:green%7C694%20Front%20Street%2022949&sensor=false">
16
17        </div>
18      </div>
19      <div data-role="footer" data-position="fixed">
20        <h4 align="center">Contact AdventureWorks</h4>
21          <div align="center" data-role="controlgroup" data-mini="true" data-type="horizontal">
22            <a href="tel:4345551212" data-role="button">Call</a>
23            <a href="http://www.trainingforce.com/" data-role="button">Web</a>
24            <a href="mailto:info@trainingforce.com" data-role="button">Email</a>
25          </div>
26      </div>
27  </div>
```

AdventureWorksApp\app\Company\index.erb

      iii. Save and close the file. Files that have unsaved changes are noted by a * on the file's tab.

           WARNING: A RhoMobile project may have multiple files named index.erb, show.erb, etc. Hovering over the tab in the IDE will display the file's full path.

    b.   Update the Company Model Controller.

        i.   Open **\app\Company\company_controller.rb**.

        ii.   Delete all existing code.

        iii.   Write code for company_controller.rb.

            1.   Because there is a single view, associated with static data, the only method necessary is *index*.

```
1    require 'rho/rhocontroller'
2    require 'helpers/browser_helper'
3
4    class CompanyController < Rho::RhoController
5      include BrowserHelper
6
7      def index
8        render :action => :index
9      end
10
11   end
```

AdventureWorksApp\app\Company\company_controller.rb

        iv.   Save and close the file.

c. Now that the Company model and view is complete, update the Application's Index page.
    i. Identify the <li> element within the page content:

```
19      <li><a href="#">Add link here...</a></li>
```

    ii. Create the link to the Company Model's Index view using *url_for.*

```
19      <li><a href="<%= url_for(:controller => :Company,  :action => :index) %>">
Company</a></li>
```

3. Run the code in a simulated mobile device.
    a. Use the Debug pull-down to select "Debug Configurations"

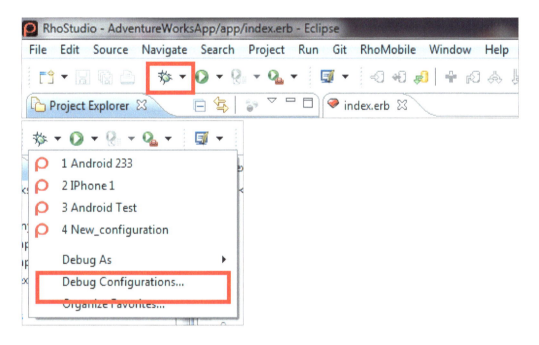

    b. The Debug Configuration window opens.

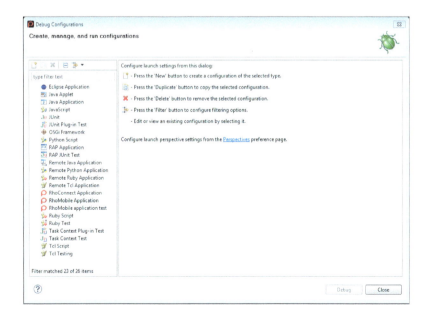

c. Select RhoMobile Application in the left pane, and click the icon for a New Configuration.

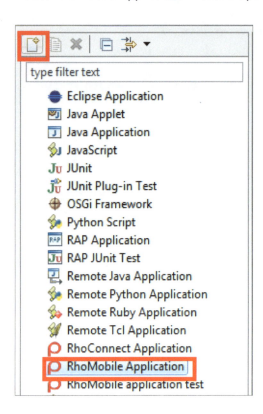

d. Type "AdventureWorks Android 2.3.3" as the Configuration Name.
    Select "AdventureWorksApp" using **[Browse]**.
    Select "Android" as the Platform, and "2.3.3" as the Android OS Version.
    Be sure "Clean before build" and "Reload application code" are selected.

e. Select **[Apply]** to save the configuration.

f. Select **[Debug]** to run the configuration in Debugging Mode.
    i. The environment perspective changes to debugging.
    ii. The application simulator opens in a separate window.
    iii. The RhoMobile Web Inspector opens in a separate window.

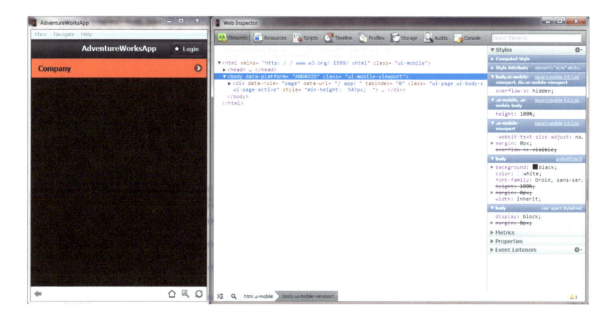

    iv. The log is an extremely useful tool. To open the log, select 'Main', 'View Log' from within the simulated application.

    v. Right-clicking in the simulated application brings up a context menu:

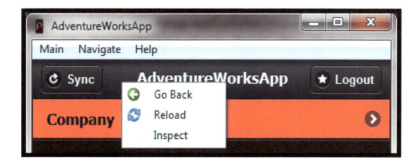

vi. The log displays detailed information about what is happening in the application.

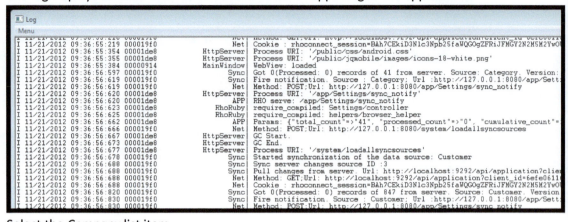

vii. Select the *Company* list item.

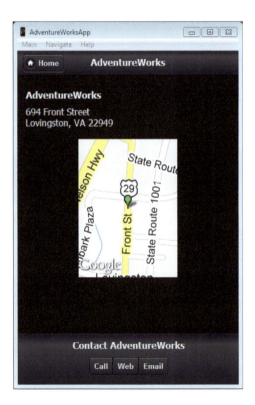

viii. After reviewing your work in the simulator, close the simulator. The Web Inspector and log (if open) close automatically.

Exercise 4: Make it Functional

In Exercise 2, the Model and View were created to display information about AdventureWorks on the application's main index page. Because a sales representative (the application's end-user) may need to access this information from any point in the application, make it available as part of the application's menu. Disable the native Android toolbar to improve usability.

1. Edit **AdventureWorksApp\app\application.rb**.

    a. Lines 8 and 9 are where the native Android toolbar can be disabled.

    ```
    8    #To remove default toolbar uncomment next line:
    9    #@@toolbar = nil
    ```

    Toggle the comment tag for Line 9. This can be done by deleting the tag, using "Source", "Uncomment" from the menu, or using the **[CTRL] – [/]** shortcut.

    ```
    8    #To remove default toolbar uncomment next line:
    9    @@toolbar = nil
    ```

    b. Establish the Default Menu options by adding code to **application.rb**. Insert the following code beginning at Line 12. Line 13 adds the direct link to the *Company* view directly from the application's main menu. Line 14 adds a link directly to the home page.

    ```
    12   @default_menu = {
    13       "About" => '/app/Company',
    14       "Home" => '/app',
    15       "Settings" => '/app/Settings',
    16       "View Log" => :log,
    17       "Exit" => :close
    18   }
    ```

2. Test the application. The AdventureWorks Android 2.3.3 Configuration is now available directly from the "Debug" drop-down. Be sure to close all open files after testing your application.

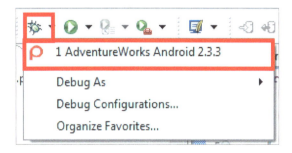

3. The RhoMobile and Debugging views within the Eclipse IDE are dramatically different. Developers can rapidly switch between views using the buttons on the top-right of the main window.

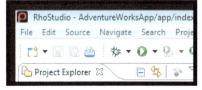

Module 2
Background

RhoConnect manages your application's connection to enterprise business systems. Module 2 creates the necessary RhoConnect application. There are four specific exercises in this Module:

- Create the RhoConnect Application
- Create the Client Source Adapter
- Starting Redis and RhoConnect
- Updating the RhoMobile Application

Outcome

Connect the mobile application to a remote data source using RhoConnect and the data source's web service.

Exercise 1: Create the RhoConnect Application

In this Exercise, the mobile application's base structure is created.

1. Start RhoMobile Suite, if not already running.
2. Go to the "File" menu.
3. Select "New", "Project". The New Project wizard starts.
4. From the list of New Project Wizards, open the RhoMobile Folder. Select "RhoConnect Application" and select **[Next]**.

5. Type "AdventureWorksProvider" in the "Project name" text field.
    Be sure "Create application in default workspace" is checked.
    Select **[Finish]**.

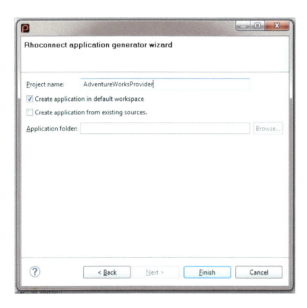

6. The Wizard creates the RhoConnect application framework in Project Explorer.
    Review the created file structure.

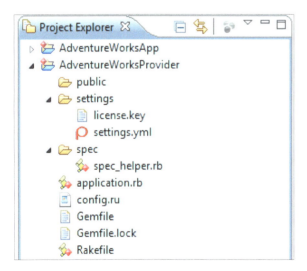

Exercise 2: Create the Customer Source Adapter

In this Exercise, a Source Adapter is created. The adapter will retrieve information using a web service call to our enterprise data source.

1. Create the Adapter in the RhoConnect Application
    a. Right-click on the "AdventureWorksProvider" folder in Project Explorer.
    b. Select 'New', 'RhoConnect Source Adapter'

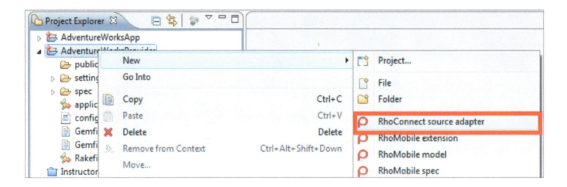

    c. Type "Customer" in the 'Source Adapter name' text field.
        Select **[Finish]**.

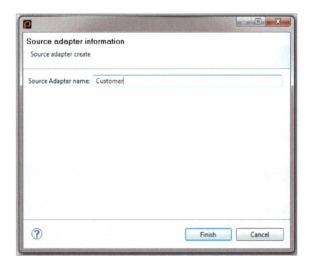

    d. Your RhoConnect application is updated.
        A "sources" folder is added with a *customer.rb* file.
        A "sources" subfolder is added to the "spec" folder with a *customer_spec.rb* file.

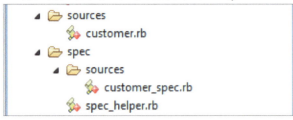

2. Update the RhoConnect Application.

a. Update the code.
    i. Open **AdventureWorksProvider\application.rb**.
    ii. Highlight all existing code and delete.
    iii. Write the Application code.

```
1  require 'xmlsimple'
2  require 'open-uri'
3
4  class Application < Rhoconnect::Base
5    class << self
6      def authenticate(username,password,session)
7        #Log in to web service and retrieve token
8        base_url = 'http://aw.oaktree-systems.com/Service.asmx/'
9
10       # Call the web service and open up the XML response
11       xml_response = open(base_url + "Authenticate?userName=#{username}&password=#{password}").read
12
13       # Read the response
14       val = XmlSimple.xml_in(xml_response)
15       token = val["content"]
16
17       # If the token is not valid (error returned), return the value as an error message
18       # Raising different error types does not appear to affect the error_code of 2
19       # returned to the callback function in the params.
20       raise token if token.start_with?("Error")
21
22       # save the token for later use in the source adapter
23       Store.put_value("username:#{username}:token",token)
24
25       return true
26     end
27
28     # Add hooks for application startup here
29     # Don't forget to call super at the end!
30     def initializer(path)
31       super
32     end
33
34     # Calling super here returns rack tempfile path:
35     # i.e. /var/folders/J4/J4wGJ-r6H7S313GEZ-Xx5E+++TI
36     # Note: This tempfile is removed when server stops or crashes...
37     # See http://rack.rubyforge.org/doc/Multipart.html for more info
38     #
39     # Override this by creating a copy of the file somewhere
40     # and returning the path to that file (then don't call super!):
41     # i.e. /mnt/myimages/soccer.png
42     def store_blob(object,field_name,blob)
43       super #=> returns blob[:tempfile]
44     end
45   end
46 end
47
48 class SourceAdapter
49
50 # Extend the SourceAdapter to include a login routine so it isn't required in every source
51   def call_service(call,params=nil)
52     val = ""
53     params = "" if params.nil?
54     url = get_service + call + "?token=" + get_token + params
55
56     # Try to call the web service and open up the XML response
```

```
57      begin
58        xml_response = open(url).read
59      rescue Exception => e
60        raise "Unable to read XML response for call: #{call}. URL: #{url}. Details: #{e.message}. Trace:
#{e.backtrace}"
61      end
62
63      # Read the response
64      # Must do this in a separate step in case the response is large
65      begin
66        val = XmlSimple.xml_in(xml_response)
67      rescue Exception => e
68        raise "Error while parsing the XML response for call: #{call}. URL: #{url}. Details: #{e.message}.
Trace: #{e.backtrace}"
69      end
70      return val
71    end
72
73    def get(tbl,col)
74      # Read the value from the Web Service XML response
75      begin
76        value = tbl[col][0]
77        # If it is an empty hash, the Web Service passed back an empty string
78        value = "" if value.to_s == "{}"
79      return value
80      rescue
81        raise "Service column '#{col}' errored out.  It probably does not exist."
82      end
83    end
84
85    def get_service
86      return 'http://aw.oaktree-systems.com/Service.asmx/'
87    end
88
89    def get_token
90      return Store.get_value("username:#{current_user.login}:token")
91    end
92
93    def is_token_valid?
94      val = call_service("IsTokenValid")
95      return val["content"].to_bool
96    end
97  end
98
99  class String
100     # Add to_bool call to the base String object type
101     def to_bool
102       begin
103         return true if self == true || self =~ (/(true|t|yes|y|1)$/i)
104         return false if self == false || self.nil? || self =~ (/(false|f|no|n|0)$/i)
105       rescue
106       end
107       raise ArgumentError.new("Invalid value for Boolean: \"#{self}\"")
108     end
109   end
110
111   Application.initializer(ROOT_PATH)
112
113   # Support passenger smart spawning/fork mode:
114   if defined?(PhusionPassenger)
115   PhusionPassenger.on_event(:starting_worker_process) do |forked|
116     if forked
117       # We're in smart spawning mode.
```

```
118      Store.db.client.reconnect
119    else
120      # We're in conservative spawning mode. We don't need to do anything.
121    end
122  end
123 end
```

AdventureWorksProvider\application.rb

iv.   Save and close the file. Files that have unsaved changes are noted by a * on the file's tab.

WARNING: A RhoMobile project will typically have multiple files named index.erb, show.erb, etc. Hovering over the tab in the IDE will display the file's full path.

3. Update the Customer Source Adapter.

   a.   Open **AdventureWorksProvider\sources\customer.rb** .

   b.   Add the code for the updated login and web service query.

```
def login
  # The login routine was changed in application.rb
  raise SourceAdapterLoginException.new("1000") if !is_token_valid?
end

def query(params=nil)
  @result = {}

  # Query the web service using the call_service method defined in application.rb
  customers = call_service("GetCustomers")
  if !customers["Customer"].nil?
    customers["Customer"].each do |c|
      customer = {}
      customer["companyname"] = get(c,'CompanyName')
      customer["customerid"] = get(c,'CustomerID')
      customer["email"] = get(c,'Email')

      # Store the value that is returned
      @result[customer["customerid"]] = customer
    end
  end
end
```

   c.   Save and close the file.

d. Verify contents of the **AdventureWorksProvider\spec\sources\customer_spec.rb** file.

```
 1  require File.join(File.dirname(__FILE__),'..','spec_helper')
 2
 3  describe "Customer" do
 4    it_should_behave_like "SpecHelper" do
 5      before(:each) do
 6        setup_test_for Customer,'testuser'
 7      end
 8
 9      it "should process Customer query" do
10        pending
11      end
12
13      it "should process Customer create" do
14        pending
15      end
16
17      it "should process Customer update" do
18        pending
19      end
20
21      it "should process Customer delete" do
22        pending
23      end
24    end
25  end
```

AdventureWorksProvider\spec\sources\customer_spec.rb

e. Verify the contents of the **AdventureWorksProvider\settings\settings.yml** file.

```
 1 #Sources
 2 :sources:
 3   Customer:
 4     :poll_interval: 300
 5
 6 :development:
 7   :licensefile: settings/license.key
 8   :redis: localhost:6379
 9   :syncserver: http://localhost:9292/api/application/
10 :test:
11   :licensefile: settings/license.key
12   :redis: localhost:6379
13   :syncserver: http://localhost:9292/api/application/
14 :production:
15   :licensefile: settings/license.key
16   :redis: localhost:6379
17   :syncserver: http://localhost:9292/api/application/
18
```

AdventureWorksProvider\settings\settings.yml

4. Update **AdventureWorksApp\rhoconfig.txt.**

    a. The location of the local server must be specified. In the file created by the wizard, the syncserver is unspecified.

```
48  # sync server url, typically this will look like 'http://<hostname>:<port>/application'
49  # for example: 'http://localhost:9292/application'
50  syncserver = ''
```

Update the file to:

```
48  # sync server url, typically this will look like 'http://<hostname>:<port>/application'
49  # for example: 'http://localhost:9292/application'
50  syncserver = 'http://localhost:9292/api/application'
```

    b. By default, a network timeout is set to 30 seconds.

```
34  # timeout of network requests in seconds (30 by default)
35  # net_timeout = 30
```

The amount of data during the initial sync is rather large. Therefore, the normal timeout of 30 seconds needs to be extended to 120 for this demonstration application. Update the file to:

```
34  # timeout of network requests in seconds (30 by default)
35  net_timeout = 120
```

Important Note: The "New", "RhoConnect Source Adapter" Wizard can intermittently fail when creating subsequent Source Adapters. In those cases, simply copy one of your existing adapters and edit the code. Remember to create a 'spec' file and update the settings.yml file, also.

Exercise 3: Starting Redis and RhoConnect

Now that you've created the adapter to retrieve and store data from your enterprise system, you need to start the application.

1. Confirm that the GEM versions installed are correct. From the Ruby command line, navigate to the AdventureWorksProvider and AdventureWorksApp directories. Type "Gem List" to view the gems that are currently in each local directory. Confirm that any listed Gems are in agreement with versions specified in **AdventureWorksProvider\Gemfile.**

   a. The XML Simple Gem is required for the AdventureWorks application. Prior to running the application, the Gem must be installed. To install the XML Simple Gem:

      i. Start a Command Prompt with Ruby. Open the Ruby folder, and select "Start Command Prompt with Ruby".

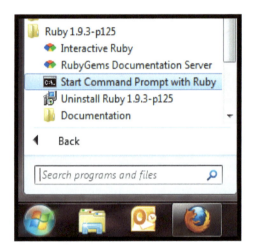

      ii. Type "gem install xml-simple –v 1.1.1" and the gem will install.

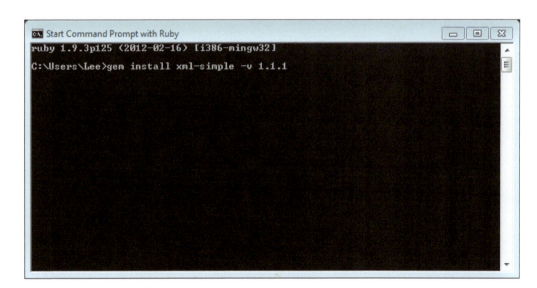

b. For developers using the Developer Install file, the following is representative of a known working configuration of Gems, and the resulting **AdventureWorksProvider\Gemfile:**

Note the addition of lines 5 and 6, referencing the XML-simple Gem installed manually in (a), above.

```
1   source 'http://rubygems.org'
2
3   gem 'rhoconnect', '3.2.0'
4
5   # For XML file parsing
6   gem 'xml-simple', '1.1.1'
7
8   # Helps with some of the limitations of green threads, not needed in ruby 1.9.x
9   gem 'SystemTimer', '~> 1.2.3', :platforms => :ruby_18
10  gem 'win32-process', :platforms => [:mswin, :mingw]
11
12  # use thin and eventmachine everywhere except JRuby
13  platforms :ruby, :ruby_19, :mingw, :mingw_19 do
14    gem "eventmachine", "~> 1.0.0.beta"
15    # using thin by default
16    gem 'thin'
17  end
18
19  # for async framework
20  # for Async, Eventful execution
21  platforms :ruby_19, :mingw_19 do
22    gem 'rack-fiber_pool'
23    gem 'async-rack'
24  end
25
26  platforms :jruby do
27    gem 'jdbc-sqlite3', ">= 3.7.2"
28    gem 'dbi', ">= 0.4.5"
29    gem 'dbd-jdbc', ">= 0.1.4"
30    gem 'jruby-openssl', ">= 0.7.4"
31    gem 'trinidad'
32    gem 'warbler'
33  end
34
35  gem 'sqlite3', ">= 1.3.3", :platforms => [:ruby, :mswin, :mingw]
36
37  group :development do
38    gem 'rhomobile-debug', ">= 1.0.2"
39  end
40
41  group :test do
42    gem 'rack-test', '>= 0.5.3', :require => "rack/test"
43    gem 'rspec', '~> 2.6.0'
44    gem 'rhomobile-debug', ">= 1.0.2"
45  end
```

2. Start the RhoConnect application to serve your data.
   a. Using a Ruby command line:
      i. Find the workspace directory for the project. The workspace directory can be found by navigating to 'Window', 'Preferences', 'General', 'Startup and Shutdown', 'Workspaces'.

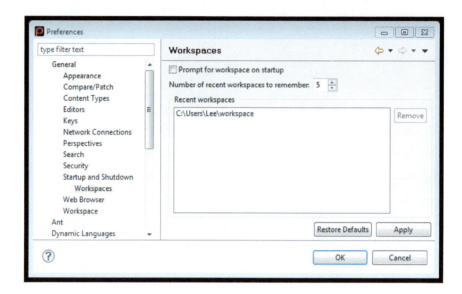

      ii. Start a Command Prompt with Ruby. Open the Ruby folder, and select "Start Command Prompt with Ruby".

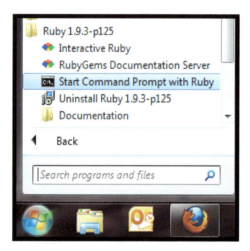

      iii. Navigate to the workspace directory identified in (i), above.

      iv. Type 'rhoconnect redis-start', [Enter]. You will see a message "Starting redis in a new window . . ." and a new window will open. If an error is encountered, look for "Could not find XXXX". That statement means that a Gem is either missing or an incorrect version is referenced. From the command prompt, type 'Gem install XXXX'. **[Shift] – [↑]** (Shift – up arrow) scrolls through previously typed commands. Gems are described by name and version number; additional characters after the specific version may be omitted.

For example: RhoConnect displays the error message "Could not find rake-0.9.5" The install command would be "gem install rake –v 0.9.5". If the version includes a trailing hyphen, as in "eventmachine-1.0.0.rc.4-x86-mingw32", the trailing information should be omitted. The correct install command would be "gem install eventmachine –v 1.0.0.rc.4".

    v.   Type 'rhoconnect start', **[Enter]**. RhoConnect starts in the current window. Redis will start in a new window. A separate window will open, displaying Redis status. The desired message is "1 clients connected".

    vi.   The RhoConnect status should update after Redis has started and successfully connected.

    vii.   Stop the RhoConnect application:
        1.   Open a Ruby command prompt and navigate to the appropriate workspace.
        2.   Type 'rhoconnect stop', **[Enter]**.
        3.   Type 'rhoconnect redis-stop', **[Enter]**.
        4.   Close the windows or type 'exit' and press **[Enter]**.

3. In the normal development process, developers will be stopping and restarting RhoConnect frequently. To facilitate this process, the **Developer RhoMobile.bat** file allows quick access to a number of functions without resorting to command line functions. This file can exist in each RhoConnect project workspace, allowing a developer to rapidly switch between active projects.
    a. Create the Developer RhoMobile.bat file found in Appendix A, page 95. Open the Developer RhoMobile batch file and edit for the current project.
        i. Line 7: Update the value to the correct Rhodes Workspace path.
           Ex: (set rhoAppPath=c:\workspace\)

ii. Line 10: Update the value for the RhoConnect Project.
Ex: (set rhoConnectProject=AdventureWorksProvider)

iii. Save the batch file.

b. Start the Developer RhoMobile Batch File

i. The Developer RhoMobile opens a menu window.

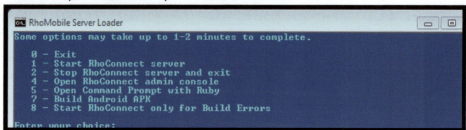

ii. Press '1' to start RhoConnect Server.

A startup message will be displayed.

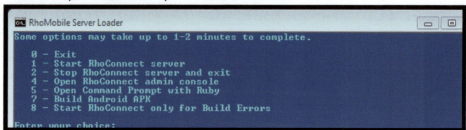

iii. A separate window will open, displaying Redis status.

iv. A separate window will open, displaying RhoConnect status.

Exercise 4: Update Your RhoMobile Application

Now that we've established the connection to the "back end" customer data, we need to add that information to the Mobile Application.

1. First, add a "Customer" model using the techniques learned in Module 1.
   a. Delete the files unique to Blackberry devices (*.bb.erb).
2. Activate synchronization with the RhoConnect Source Adapter.
   a. Enable synchronization in the Customer model.
      i. Open **AdventureWorksApp\app\Customer\customer.rb**.
      ii. Uncomment line 7.

```
6    # Uncomment the following line to enable sync with Customer.
7    enable :sync
```

3. Update the application.
   a. Add a link to open the customer's list to the application's main page.
      (**AdventureWorksApp\app\index.erb**). This will be a list item.

```
20   <li><a href="<%= url_for(:controller => :Customer, :action => :index) %>">
     Customers</a></li>
```

   b. Update the **AdventureWorksApp\app\Customer\index.erb** file. This displays the list of all customers.
      When the Model Wizard generated the Customer model and used the placeholder attribute 'a', that
      value propagated to each sub-page (index, edit, show).

i. First, look at the header div. The end user will not be allowed to add customers to the enterprise data source, so the header div can be revised to:

```
<div data-role="header" data-position="inline">
    <h1>Customers</h1>
      <a href="<%= Rho::RhoConfig.start_path %>" class="ui-btn-left" data-icon="home" data-direction="reverse" <%= "data-ajax='false'" if is_bb6 %>>
        Home
      </a>
</div>
```

ii. The Wizard generated basic code within the content area of the page as well:
1. A *do* loop, adding each customer as a list item.
2. An `<a href>` link to the *:show* function and page wrapping each list item.
3. The actual list item, `<%= @customer.a %>` This needs to be updated this list item to reflect actual variable returned from the database.

```
<div data-role="content">
    <ul data-role="listview">
      <% @customers.each do |customer| %>
          <li> <a href="<%= url_for(:action => :show, :id => customer.object) %>">
                <%= customer.companyname %></a>
          </li>
        <% end %>
    </ul>
</div>
```

c. Update the **AdventureWorksApp\app\Customer\show.erb** file. This file displays the information on the individual customer.

i. Update the heading. Leave the **[Back]** and **[Edit]** buttons in place. The Edit function will be created in Module 4.

Replace `<%= @customer.a %>` with static text: `Customer Details.`

```
<div data-role="header" data-position="inline">
    <h1>Customer Detail</h1>
```

ii. Replace the page content. On the page generated by the wizard, each variable is displayed as a list item.

```
<ul data-role="listview">
  <li>
      <div class="itemLabel">A</div>
      <div class="itemValue"><%= @customer.a %></div>
  </li>
</ul>
```

You should update the code to remove the "listview" and display the information on the customer as a static page:

```
<div data-role="content">
    <h1><%= @customer.companyname %></h1>
    <div>
        Customer ID: <%= @customer.customerid %><br/>
        Email: <%= @customer.email %>
    </div>
</div>
```

4. Run the Mobile Application from the Debugging drop-down. Be sure RhoConnect is running prior to starting the mobile application. You will need to log in to the application using the supplied credentials. To log in, select **[Login]** in the upper right corner of the application. Enter the following credentials:
   a. Login: Training1Instance
   b. Password: Learning2Day
   c. Select **[Login]**.

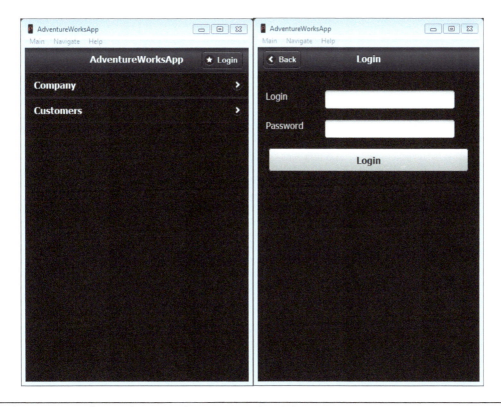

Note: When running the application, the Login credentials are:

User: Training1Instance   **Password: Learning2Day**

5. Authentication relies on a token created via the web service when the user logs in. This token changes each day.
   a. Create a new model called *Session*. For review of model creation, see page 11.
   b. Delete all the files in **AdventureWorksApp\app\session** EXCEPT **session.rb**.

6. Open **AdventureWorksApp\application.rb.**
    a. Edit the code beginning at line 21. Insert lines 23 – 45.

    This code forces the "log out" of the user if the day has changed.

```
21   SyncEngine.set_notification(-1, "/app/Settings/sync_notify", '')
22
23 # Web Service Token becomes invalid after a day.  Auto-logout before syncing each day.
24 # Otherwise, we get errors on every sync call because the token stored
25 # in the RhoConnect Redis instance is invalid.
26    @session = Session.find(:first) # single row in sync database
27    current_date = Time.new
28    day_of_year = current_date.yday
29    if @session.nil?
30      # Initialize a new instance and set the default values
31      @session = Session.create('last_load' => day_of_year)
32    else
33      if SyncEngine::logged_in == 1
34        # Log out if the day changed. The token is invalid
35        # We have to reauthenticate for a new token
36        SyncEngine.logout if day_of_year != @session.last_load.to_i
37      end
38    end
39
40    # Regardless of whether the user is logged in, update the session flag so
41    # we know the last day that the application was accessed.
42    # When the user logs in, it is correct, and the user won't get logged out
43    # on the next load.
44    @session.last_load = day_of_year
45    @session.save
```

7. When running the application simulator for the first time each day, the user will need to select [Login] and enter the credentials provided in (4.), above.

Module 3

Background

In Modules 1 and 2, a Mobile Application was created then connected it to an enterprise data source. In this Module the application will be improved and deployed on an Android mobile device. There are five exercises:

- Edit the Customer Source Adapter
- Modify the Customer Controller
- Modify the Customer Views
- Update the Application Brand & Identity
- Build and Deploy a Production Version of the Application

Outcome

Deploy a functional mobile application.

Exercise 1: Edit the Customer Source Adapter

In Module 2, only the customer's company name, client ID number, and e-mail address were requested. The web service has much more information available for use.

1. Stop Redis and RhoConnect, if running. This can be done by pressing option "2" from the Developer RhoMobile batch file or by typing "rhoconnect stop" and "rhoconnect redis-stop" from the Ruby command line (option 5).
2. Open **AdventureWorksProvider\sources\customer.rb**
   a. Use the following table as a guide for retrieving additional data from the web service. Each new line should appear after line 20:

```
customer["applicationvariable"] = get(c,'WebServiceVariable')
```

Application Variable Name	Web Service Variable
addressline1	AddressLine1
addressline2	AddressLine2
City	City
Country	Country
Firstname	FirstName
Lastname	LastName
Middlename	MiddleName
Namesuffix	NameSuffix
Phone	Phone
Photo	Photo
Postalcode	PostalCode
Salutation	Salutation
State	State

   b. Save and close the **AdventureWorksProvider\sources\customer.rb**.

3. Start RhoConnect using the Developer RhoMobile batch file. If RhoConnect fails to start, look for typographical errors. Option 8 on the Developer RhoMobile batch menu assists in debugging these types of errors.

Exercise 2: Modify the Views

The view created in Module 2 is relatively simple. Now that more information about each customer is available, work on refining the Index and Show views. Create an index view that lists the customers by name and organization, and also shows a thumbnail photograph. Update the *show* view so that the user has all the information available, plus allows the user to place a call to or email a customer directly from the mobile device.

1. To only display fields if information is returned by the database, i.e. don't display empty placeholders, a helper method can be created. Add a method called *blank?* to the browser_helper.rb file.

    a. Open **AdventureWorksApp\app\Helpers\browser_helper.rb**.

    b. Add the following code:

    ```
    def blank?(value)
       value.nil? || value == "" || value.length==0
    end
    ```

    c. Save and close the file.

2. Open **AdventureWorksApp\app\Customer\index.erb**.

    a. In the content section:

        i. Add the ability to filter the list using JQuery Mobile. Add `data-filter="true"` to the list.

        ```
        <ul data-role="listview" data-filter="true">
        ```

        ii. Update the list item to show the customer's photo. If the customer doesn't have a photo, display a default image.

            1. Ensure the file "portrait.gif" is located in the **AdventureWorksApp\public\images\custom** directory. This file is included with the downloaded Android icons from Module 1.

            2. Add code within the list item (<li>) to display the photo if one is found. Note the use of the *!blank?* method created in step 1.

            ```
            <% if !blank?(customer.photo) %>
                 <img style="height:54px;" src="<%= customer.photo %>">
              <% else %>
                 <img style="height: 54px;" src='/../public/images/custom/portrait.gif'>
            <% end %>
            ```

            3. Add code for the customer's name and company.

            ```
            <%= "#{customer.lastname},#{customer.firstname} #{customer.middlename}" %> <br/>
            <%= customer.companyname %>
            ```

b. Save the file and run the simulation to see the results.

3. Open **AdventureWorksApp\app\Customer\show.erb**.
   a. In the content section:
      i. Decide on a format for the view. Create a div or table to display a larger version of the photograph and the customer's name. Two possible formats are shown below:

Format A

← 100 % →

Photo (80 px square)
Customer Name Customer Company Name

Format B

← 45% →   ← 55% →

Photo (80 px square)	Customer Name Customer Company Name

      ii. Write the code for the view.

1. Modify the content divs. First, include the customer's photo if available.

```
<div style="width:100%; vertical-align: middle; text-align: center">
  <% if !blank?(@customer.photo)%>
    <img style="height:80px;" src="<%= @customer.photo %>">
  <% else %>
    <img style="height:80px;" src="/../public/images/custom/portrait.gif">
  <% end %>
</div>

<div style="width:100%; vertical align: middle; text-align: center">
  <h3><%= @customer.firstname %> <%= @customer.middlename %> <%= @customer.lastname %>
  </h3>
  <% if !blank?(@customer.companyname) %>
    <%= @customer.companyname %>
  <% end %>
</div>
```

2. Create a section to display the customer's address.

```
<div style="width:100%; vertical-align: middle; text-align: left">
  <% if !blank?(@customer.address1)%>
    <%= @customer.address1 %>
  <% end %>
  <% if !blank?(@customer.address2)%>
    <%= @customer.address2 %>
  <% end %>
  <% if ( !blank?(@customer.city) && !blank?(@customer.state) )%>
    <%= @customer.city %>, <%= @customer.state %> <%= @customer.postalcode %>
  <% end %>
</div>
```

3. Create a section to display the customer's e-mail and telephone numbers.
   Display an icon that allows the user to e-mail / call the customer using one touch.

```
<div>
  <table style="width:100%">
    <tr>
      <td style="width:80%, vertical-align:middle, text-align:left">
        <% if blank?(@customer.phone) %>
          No Phone Associated with Customer
        <% else %>
          <h1>Telephone:</h1>
          <%= @customer.phone %>
        <% end %>
      </td>
      <td style="width:20%, vertical-align:middle, text-align:right">
        <% if !blank?(@customer.phone) %>
          <a href="tel:<%= @customer.phone %>">
          <img src="/../public/images/custom/call.png"></a>
        <% end %>
      </td>
    </tr>
    <tr>
```

```
<td style="width:80%, vertical-align:middle, text-align:left">
  <% if blank?(@customer.email) %>
    No Email Associated with Customer
  <% else %>
    <h1>E-mail:</h1>
    <%= @customer.email %>
  <% end %>
</td>
<td style="width:20%, vertical-align:middle, text-align:right">
  <% if !blank?(@customer.email) %>
    <a href="mailto:<%= @customer.email %>">
    <img src="/../public/images/custom/email.png"></a>
  <% end %>
</td>
  </tr>
  </table>
</div>
```

b. Save and close the file. Run the application using the Debug drop-down to view the updated application.

Exercise 3: Modify the Customer Controller

1. Open **AdventureWorksApp\app\Customer\customer_controller.rb**.
2. The current code for the existing *index* function simply returns the list in unsorted form. Update the controller to alphabetize the customer list based on last name.

```
def index
   @customers =Customer.find(:all, :order => 'lastname')
end
```

3. Save the file and run the application. Select "Customers" and scroll downward.   Notice how the default sorting differentiates between last names that are upper case and lower case. You need to edit the controller file a bit more to provide the user with a true alphabetical list, regardless of case.

```
def index
   @customers =Customer.find(:all, :order => 'lastname') do |x,y|
      x.downcase <=> y.downcase
   end
end
```

Exercise 4: Update the Application's Identity and Brand

Deploying a mobile application is an extension of an organization's brand. There are two basic components that help communicate that brand. First, the "loading" screen that appears when you first install and launch the program. Second, the application icon that appears on the user's device. Visit the Android, iPhone, or Blackberry developer web site for tips on icon design.

1. Import the image "loading.png" from the AdventureWorks Branding Folder from Oak Tree's RhoMobile Dropbox site into the **AdventureWorksApp\app** directory. Be sure the correct folder is selected. Select "Overwrite existing resources without warning". Select **[Finish]**.

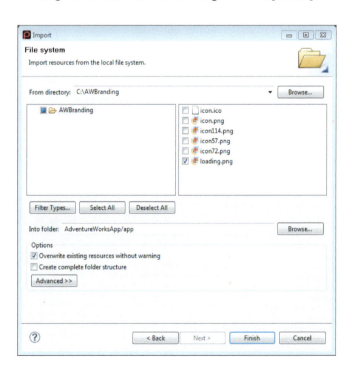

2. Import the remaining files from AdventureWorks Branding Folder into the **AdventureWorksApp\icon** directory. Be sure the correct destination folder is selected. Select "Overwrite existing resources without warning". Select **[Finish]**. A total of five (5) files are essential:
   a. Icon.ico
   b. Icon.png
   c. Icon57.png (57 x 57, 24-bit, non-interlaced)
   d. Icon72.png (72 x 72, 24-bit, non-interlaced)
   e. Icon114.png (114 x 114, 24-bit, non-interlaced)

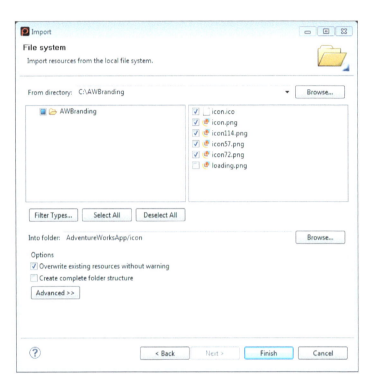

Exercise 5: Build and Deploy a Functional Application

1. An easy way to test a functional build is to use an Android device. The provided batch files allow for easy creation of production Android build.

    a. The Android Software Development Kit (SDK) and Native Development Kit (NDK) should be installed. Specify the location of the SDK and NDK files in RhoMobile Suite by navigating to 'Windows', 'Preferences', 'RhoMobile', 'Android'. To obtain the Android SDK and NDK, visit http://developer.android.com/sdk/index.html.

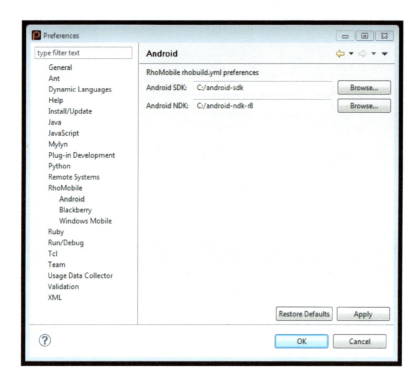

    b. Select option 7 from the batch file menu.

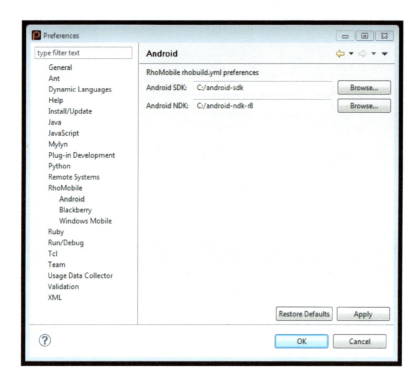

c. The Batch file requests the Project's Name. Type "AdventureWorksApp".

```
RhoMobile Server Loader
Project name in workspace: AdventureWorksApp
```

d. A status screen will appear.

```
RhoMobile Server Loader
Project name in workspace: AdventureWorksApp
APK location: C:\Users\Lee\workspace\AdventureWorksApp\bin\target\android
Starting APK build...

Some options may take up to 1-2 minutes to complete.
    0 - Exit
    1 - Start RhoConnect server
    2 - Stop RhoConnect server and exit
    4 - Open RhoConnect admin console
    5 - Open Command Prompt with Ruby
    7 - Build Android APK
    8 - Start RhoConnect only for Build Errors
```

e. The finished APK file can be found in the **\bin\target\android** directory. From there, it can be copied to an Android device using the device's USB cable, or by deploying to a file sharing site. <u>Go to the Settings, Application, Settings and check the box to allow installation from "Unknown Sources" in order to install to your device. Remember to return this to the original setting after installing your file to ensure security of the device.</u>

2. A production build may also be initiated by selecting 'RhoMobile', 'Production Build'.

Module 4

Background

In this Module the application will be expanded. Instead of just viewing data from the server, the mobile application will be used to manipulate and update the information.

- Paginate the Customers view.
- Use the mobile application to update a customer phone number.
- Create a detailed product structure.
- Retrieve a customer's order history and product detail.
- Create a sale to a customer.

Outcome

Expand the functionality of the mobile application to include manipulating server data.

Exercise 1: Paginate the Customer View

In Module 2 and 3, customer information was requested. There are a large number of records in the AdventureWorks database. Although the end user could conceivably scroll down through the entire list, or use the filter box to view only certain records, there may be occasions a developer wants to implement paging of data.

1. Open **AdventureWorksApp\app\customer\customer_controller.rb**.

2. Add methods to facilitate paging.
   a. Define *paged_index*. This is the method called initially from the application index screen.

```
def paged_index
    #Locate the first record
    @customers = Customer.find(:first)

    #Set the initial values for the page number, records per page variables, and visibility of the
    #  show more button.
    @page = 0
    @per_page = 15
    @show_more_button = true


    #Set a variable to control the previous button on the first page of records.
    #The .to_i method ensures the string is converted to an integer prior to comparison
    @show_less_button = false if @params['page'].to_i == 0

    #set variable from Controller using .paginate and variables; render index page.
    @customers = Customer.paginate(:page => @page, :per_page => @per_page, :order => 'lastname')
    render :action => :index
end
```

b. Define *more*

```
def more

  # After showing subsequent pages, must show less button so set it to true
  @show_less_button = true

  # Add 1 to the current page parameter, must convert to integer first.
  @page = @params['page'].to_i + 1

  # Continue current number of records on page, but must convert to integer
  @per_page = @params['per_page'].to_i

  # Set the variables to return
  @customers = Customer.paginate(:page => @page, :per_page => @per_page, :order => 'lastname')

  # Send to the view
  render :action => :index
end
```

c. Define *less*

```
def less
  # Similar to method more, only subtract one from the @page variable and do compare to determine
  # if show less button should be displayed

  @show_less_button = true
  @page = @params['page'].to_i - 1
  @per_page = @params['per_page'].to_i
  @show_less_button = false if @page == 0
  @customers = Customer.paginate(:page => @page, :per_page => @per_page, :order => 'lastname')
  render :action => :index
end
```

d. Update the *index* method to include the defined variables.

```
def index
    @customers = Customer.paginate(:page => @page, :per_page => @per_page, :order => 'lastname')
do |x,y|
      x.downcase<=>y.downcase
    end
    render :back => '/app'
end
```

e. Save and close the file

3. Open **AdventureWorksApp\app\index.erb.**
   a. Update the list item. Users need to be directed to the *paged_index* method so that the initial variables are set before calling the *index* method.

```
<div data-role="content">
    <ul data-role="listview">
      <li><a href="<%= url_for(:controller => :Company, :action => :index) %>">Company</a></li>
      <li><a href="<%= url_for(:controller => :Customer, :action => :paged_index)
%>">Customers</a></li>
    </ul>
  </div>
```

   b. Save and close the file.

4. Open **AdventureWorksApp\app\customer\index.erb.**
   a. Update the list item so that the current @page and @per_page values are passed to the *show* method. This ensures the user can navigate back to the correct page after viewing the contact.

```
<li>
  <a href="<%= url_for(:action => :show, :query => {:id => customer.object, :page => @page,
:per_page => @per_page})%>">
```

   b. Create the buttons for "More" and "Less". These will be in the footer of the application. Note the use of @show_less_button to evaluate whether the button should be displayed.

```
<div data-role="footer">
  <div data-role="controlgroup" data-type="horizontal" style="text-align: center">

  <% if @show_less_button == true %>
      <a href="<%= url_for(:action => :less, :query => {:page => @page, :per_page => @per_page})
%>" data-role="button">Previous</a>
    <% end %>
      <a href="<%= url_for(:action => :more, :query => {:page => @page, :per_page => @per_page})
%>" data-role="button">Next</a>
  </div>
</div>
```

5. Test the application.
    a. Save and close all files.
    b. Stop and restart the Redis and RhoConnect instances.
    c. Open the application in debugging mode and test the paging by going to "Customers" and using the **[Previous]** and **[Next]** buttons.

Exercise 2: Update a Customer Phone Number

One of the key benefits of working with a RhoMobile application is the ability to migrate changes to the server. In this exercise a customer phone number will be updated from the *edit* screen.

1. Open **AdventureWorksApp\app\Customer\show.erb.**

   Review the header div's code for the *Edit* button.

   ```
   8    <a href="<%= url_for(:action => :edit, :id => @customer.object) %>" class="ui-btn-right"
   data-icon="star">
   9      Edit
   10   </a>
   ```

2. Edit **AdventureWorksApp\app\Customer\edit.erb.**

   a. When the model was created by the Model Wizard, a 'Delete' button was included as part of the header for the Edit page. The end user should not be able to delete customers, so remove the code for the delete button from the header. The header should be:

   ```
   <div data-role="header" data-position="inline">
     <h1>Edit <%= @customer.a %></h1>
       <a href="<%= url_for :action => :show, :id => @customer.object %>" class="ui-btn-left" data-
   icon="back" data-direction="reverse">
       Cancel
       </a>
   </div>
   ```

   b. Edit the content div. The input methods must be contained in a form, where the action is the *update* method. Change the property references to "phone" as outlined below.

   ```
   <div data-role="content">
     <form method="POST" action="<%= url_for :action => :update %>">
       <input type="hidden" name="id" value="<%= @customer.object %>"/>
         <div data-role="fieldcontain">
           <label for="customer[phone]" class="fieldLabel">Phone</label>
           <input type="text" id="customer[phone]" name="customer[phone]" value="<%= @customer.phone
   %>" <%= placeholder( "Phone" ) %> />
         </div>
       <input type="submit" value="Update"/>
     </form>
   </div>
   ```

3. Review **AdventureWorksApp\app\Customer\customer_controller.rb**.
   a. Verify the *edit* method is accurate. The method first locates the proper record using the "id" parameter. If found, it renders the **edit.erb** file.

```
def edit
  @customer = Customer.find(@params['id'])
    if @customer
      render :action => :edit, :back => url_for(:action => :index)
    else
      redirect :action => :index
    end
end
```

   b. Verify the *update* method is accurate. The record is located using the "id" parameter, then any changed attributes (the updated phone number) are passed to the source adapter.

```
def update
  @customer = Customer.find(@params['id'])
  @customer.update_attributes(@params['customer']) if @customer
  redirect :action => :index
end
```

4. Edit the Source Adapter.
   a. Open **AdventureWorksProvider\sources\customer.rb**.
   b. Edit the *update* method.
      This defines how the hash received from the mobile device is passed back to the enterprise service.
      In this case, a web service is used. Note the use of URI::encode to ensure the data is parsed correctly.

```
def update(update_hash)
  c = update_hash
  if !c["phone"].nil?
    val =
call_service("SetCustomerPhoneNumber","&customerID=#{c["id"]}&phoneNumber=#{URI::encode(c["phone"]
)}")
    return val["content"].to_bool
  end
end
```

5. Test the application.
   a. Save and close all files.
   b. Stop and restart the Redis and RhoConnect instances.
   c. Start the mobile application using the Debugging drop-down menu.

d. Navigate to an individual record from the customer list. Select **[Edit]**. Enter a new phone number [(123) 555-1212] for the selected record and select **[Update]**. Avoid using working / real phone numbers since this information is publicly exposed.

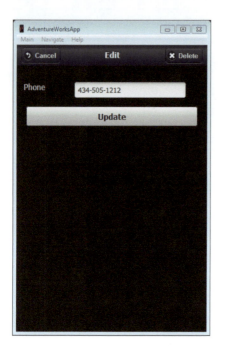

e. The updated information will be reflected on the server after the next synchronization. Remember that synchronization is done on a specific interval, so the changes may not show up on the enterprise database for 3-5 minutes.

    i. To view details on the Sync status, select *View Log* from RhoSimulator.

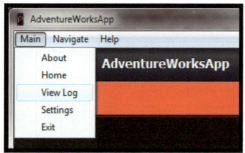

    ii. The Log opens in a new window.

        Look for lines similar to the following:

```
APP| Params: {"total_count"=>"847", "processed_count"=>"847",
"cumulative_count"=>"847", "source_id"=>"3", "source_name"=>"Customer",
"sync_type"=>"incremental", "status"=>"in_progress", "rho_callback"=>"1"}
```

        The log will show a status of "ok" and a processed record count for each synchronized data set.

The log shows detailed information on parameters being passed, errors, etc. When changes are made to Source Adapters or Controllers, open the log and review the information presented.

iii. As the updated record is processed, the passing of information back to the server is confirmed in the log:

```
APP| Params: {"total_count"=>"847", "processed_count"=>"1", "cumulative_count"=>"1",
"source_id"=>"3", "source_name"=>"Customer", "sync_type"=>"incremental",
"status"=>"ok",
```

Exercise 3: Create the Product Structure

The modified AdventureWorks database contains a large amount of information on the individual products. Before exploring orders and order details, the product information needs to be available on the device. Before creating the model-view-controller structure for products, the enterprise data structure needs to be understood.

AdventureWorks uses a category structure to define the product line:
Parent Category => Child Category (subcategory) => Product.

The list of categories is subject to change frequently. Therefore, a method exists within the web service to call a full list of categories. This information will be used within the Product model to assist with navigation, and will not require individual views.

1. Create a *Category* source adapter. Be sure the proper file is created in the /spec/ directory as well, and add the adapter to the **settings.yml** file.

    a. Once the source adapter is created, add the revised login routine and a query statement.

```ruby
def login
  raise SourceAdapterLoginException.new("1000") if !is_token_valid?
end

def query(params=nil)
  @result = {}

  # Query the web service
  categories = call_service("GetCategories")
  if !categories["Category"].nil?
    categories["Category"].each do |c|
      category = {}
      category["categoryid"] = get(c,'CategoryID')
      category["name"] = get(c,'Name')
      category["parentcategoryid"] = get(c,'ParentCategoryID')
      category["parentname"] = get(c,'ParentName')

      # Set the value that is returned
      @result[category["categoryid"]] = category
    end
  end
end
```

    b. Save and close the file

2. Create a *Product* source adapter. The products assigned to each Parent Category are called independently via the web service. The *Product* source adapter is very different from the *Customer* source adapter. The *Customer* source adapter populated a single array with data from a single web service call. The *Product* source adapter retrieves information from multiple calls (one for each parent category) and combines the data into a single array. Be sure the proper file is created in the /spec/ directory and add the adapter to the **settings.yml** file.

    a. Open **AdventureWorksProvider\sources\product.rb**

    b. Update the code by adding the following elements.

```ruby
def login
  raise SourceAdapterLoginException.new("1000") if !is_token_valid?
end

# Create a method to ensure currency is formatted correctly.
def format_currency( value, pre_symbol='$', thousands=',' )
  "#{pre_symbol}#{
    ( "%.2f" % value ).gsub(
      /(\d)(?=(?:\d{3})+(?:$|\.))/,
      "\\1#{thousands}"
    )
  }"
end

# Create a method that can be called for each Parent category
# This prevents having to duplicate this code for each method
def handle_product(p)
  product = {}
  product["categoryid"] = get(p,'CategoryID')
  product["color"] = get(p,'Color')
  product["datesellend"] = get(p,'DateSellEnd')
  product["datesellendraw"] = get(p,'DateSellEndRaw')
  product["datesellstart"] = get(p,'DateSellStart')
  product["datesellstartraw"] = get(p,'DateSellStartRaw')
  product["listprice"] = get(p,'ListPrice')
  product["listpriceraw"] = get(p,'ListPriceRaw')
  product["modelid"] = get(p,'ModelID')
  product["name"] = get(p,'Name')
  product["photo"] = get(p,'Photo')
  product["productid"] = get(p,'ProductID')
  product["productnumber"] = get(p,'ProductNumber')
  product["size"] = get(p,'Size')
  product["standardcost"] = get(p,'StandardCost')
  product["standardcostraw"] = get(p,'StandardCostRaw')

  # Add a custom field so the reps can see the profit per product
  product["profit"] = format_currency(product["listprice"].to_f - product["standardcost"].to_f)
  product["profitraw"] = product["listprice"].to_f - product["standardcost"].to_f

  # Look up taxes and shipping costs
  # Value returned looks like the following line:
  #     SubTotal: $34.99/Tax: $2.80/Shipping: $0.87/Total: $38.66
  pricing =
call_service("GetPricing","&productID=#{product["productid"]}&quantity=1&discountPercent=0")
  if !pricing["content"].start_with?("ERROR")
```

```ruby
      items = pricing["content"].split("/")
      items.each do |item|
        parts = item.split(":")

        # Only interested in the Tax and Shipping items
        if parts[0] == "Tax" || parts[0] == "Shipping"
          product["tax"] = parts[1].strip
          product["shipping"] = parts[1].strip

          amount = parts[1].split("$")
          product["taxraw"] = amount[1]

          amount = parts[1].split("$")
          product["shippingraw"] = amount[1]
        end
      end
    end
  end
  return product
end

def query(params=nil)
  @result = {}

  # Query the web service - info on the first parent category
  products = call_service("GetProductAccessories")
  if !products["Product"].nil?
    products["Product"].each do |p|
      product = handle_product(p)

      # Store the value that is returned
      @result[product["productid"]] = product
    end
  end

  # Query the web service
  products = call_service("GetProductBikes")
  if !products["Product"].nil?
    products["Product"].each do |p|
      product = handle_product(p)

      # Store the value that is returned
      @result[product["productid"]] = product
    end
  end

  # Query the web service
  products = call_service("GetProductClothing")
  if !products["Product"].nil?
    products["Product"].each do |p|
      product = handle_product(p)


      # Store the value that is returned
      @result[product["productid"]] = product
    end
```

```
  end

  # Query the web service
  products = call_service("GetProductComponents")
  if !products["Product"].nil?
    products["Product"].each do |p|
      product = handle_product(p)

      # Store the value that is returned
      @result[product["productid"]] = product
    end
  end
end

def sync
  # Manipulate @result before it is saved, or save it
  # yourself using the Rhoconnect::Store interface.
  # By default, super is called below which simply saves @result
  super
end

def logoff
  # TODO: Logout from the data source if necessary
end
end
```

c. Save and close the file.

3. Create the mobile application's *Product* and *Category* models.
    a. Since views are not required for the Category model, all .erb files may be deleted. The resulting Category model should resemble this:

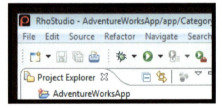

    b. In the *Product* model, the edit.erb and new.erb files may be deleted.

4. Activate synchronization for the *Category* and *Product* models.
    a. First, enable synchronization in each model.
        i. Open **AdventureWorksApp\app\Category\category.rb**.
        ii. Uncomment line 7.

```
6    # Uncomment the following line to enable sync with Category.
7    enable :sync
```

        iii. Repeat step ii in **AdventureWorksApp\app\Product\product.rb.**

5. If RhoConnect and Redis are running:

a. Stop, using either a command line command in Ruby or the RhoMobile Developer Batch file.

b. Restart RhoConnect so that the new adapters are available.

6. Update the mobile application.

   a. Add a link to open the product list to the application's main page. (**AdventureWorksApp\app\index.erb**). This will be a list item.

```
20    <li><a href="<%= url_for(:controller => :Product, :action => :index)
%>">Products</a></li>
```

   i. Save and close the file.

   b. Open **AdventureWorksApp\app\product\product_controller.rb**.

      i. Alter the index method so that it shows the master list of product categories. The 'parentcategory' field has a value of '0' for top level categories, so a :*condition* statement is applied as part of the :*find*. This ensures top-level categories are returned. No specific render is called, so the default page **AdventureWorksApp\app\product\index.erb** is rendered.

```
def index
   @categories = Category.find(
      :all,
      :order => ['name'],
      :orderdir => ['ASC'],
      :conditions => {
        {
           :name=>'parentcategoryid',
           :op=>'='
        } => '0'
      }
   )
end
```

      ii. Save **AdventureWorksApp\app\product\product_controller.rb** but leave the file open.

   c. Open **AdventureWorksApp\app\product\index.erb**.

      i. In the header div, remove the `<a href>` code for a **[New]** button.

      ii. Update the code in the content div. Note that the individual variable `category.categoryid` of the list item is passed as the :*id* when the user selects a list item.

```
<ul data-role="listview">
   <% @categories.each do |category| %>
     <li>
        <a href="<%= url_for(:action => :show_subcategory, :query => {:id =>
category.categoryid}) %>">
           <%= category.name %>
        </a>
     </li>
   <% end %>
</ul>
```

      iii. Save and close **AdventureWorksApp\app\product\index.erb**.

d. Return to **AdventureWorksApp\app\product\product_controller.rb**. Create a method called *show_subcategory.* The variable `@params['id']` contains the variable `category.categoryid` from the *index.erb* page that was just modified. Understanding the structure of the data is extremely important; this variable represents a top-level category which becomes the basis for our next query. By setting the *:condition* statement equal to the enterprise data variable `parentcategoryid`, only subcategories of the correct top-level category are returned. *Render* **AdventureWorksApp\app\product\subcategory.erb**.

```
def show_subcategory
   @categories = Category.find(
     :all,
     :order => ['name'],
     :orderdir => ['ASC'],
     :conditions => {
       {
          :name=>'parentcategoryid',
          :op=>'='
       } => @params['id']
     }
   )
   render :action => :subcategory
 end
```

  i. Save the **AdventureWorksApp\app\product\product_controller.rb** but leave it open.

  ii. Create the page **AdventureWorksApp\app\product\subcategory.erb**. Again, the variable `category.categoryid` is used to capture the selected category, so that the *:show_productlist* method can query the product data correctly.

   1. To create the file, right-click on the **AdventureWorksApp\app\Product** folder. Select 'New', 'File' and a Wizard opens.

   2. Type 'subcategory.erb' as the File Name and select **[Finish]**.

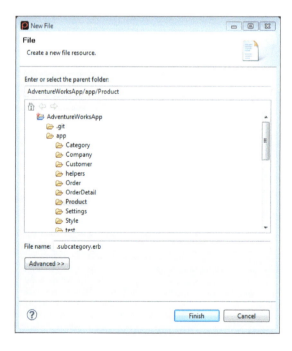

3. Open **AdventureWorksApp\app\product\subcategory.erb** for editing and write the code.

```
<div data-role="page">
  <div data-role="header" data-position="inline">
    <h1>Products</h1>
      <a href="<%= url_for :action => :index %>" class="ui-btn-left" data-icon="arrow-l"
data-direction="reverse">
      Back
      </a>
  </div>

  <div data-role="content">
    <ul data-role="listview">
      <% @categories.each do |category| %>
          <li>
            <a href="<%= url_for(:action => :show_productlist, :query => {:id =>
category.categoryid}) %>">
              <%= category.name %>
            </a>
          </li>
      <% end %>
    </ul>
  </div>
</div>
```

iii. Save and close **AdventureWorksApp\app\product\subcategory.erb.**

e. Return to **AdventureWorksApp\app\product\product_controller.rb**. Create a method called *show_productlist* to return only the desire products. Note that now, the find has shifted from Category to Product data. The variable `@params['id']` contains the query from the subcategory page, and is used to identify only products belonging to that specific category. The page **AdventureWorksApp\app\product\productlist.erb** will be rendered.

```
def show_productlist
  @products = Product.find(
    :all,
    :order => ['name'],
    :orderdir => ['ASC'],
    :conditions => {
      {
        :name=>'categoryid',
        :op=>'='
      } => @params['id']
    }
  )
  render :action => :productlist
end
```

i. Save and close **AdventureWorksApp\app\product\product_controller.rb.**

ii. Create the file **AdventureWorksApp\app\product\productlist.erb.**

    1. Create the file using the same method as subcategory.erb.

    2. Write the code for the page.

```
<div data-role="page">
  <div data-role="header" data-position="inline">
    <h1>Products</h1>
    <a href="<%= Rho::RhoConfig.start_path %>" class="ui-btn-left" data-icon="home" data-
direction="reverse" <%= "data-ajax='false'" if is_bb6 %>>
      Home
    </a>

  </div>
  <div data-role="content">
    <ul data-role="listview">
      <% @products.each do |product| %>
        <li>
          <a href="<%= url_for(:action => :show, :query => {:id =>
product.productid})%>">
            <% if !blank?(product.photo) %>
              <img style='height:54px' src='<%= product.photo %>'>
            <% else %>
              <img style='height:54px' src='/../public/images/custom/notfound.jpg'>
            <% end %>
            <h3><%= product.name %></h3>
            <%= product.color %> <%= product.listprice %>
          </a>
        </li>
      <% end %>
    </ul>
  </div>
</div>
```

iii. Save and close **AdventureWorksApp\app\product\productlist.erb.**

f. Update **AdventureWorksApp/app/product/show.erb.**

    i. Open **AdventureWorksApp/app/product/show.erb.**

    ii. Write the code.

```
<div data-role="page" data-add-back-btn="false">
  <div data-role="header" data-position="inline">
    <h1>Product Details</h1>
    <a href="<%= url_for :action => :index %>" class="ui-btn-left" data-icon="arrow-l"
data-direction="reverse">
      Back
  </div>
  <div data-role="content">
    <ul data-role="listview">
        <li><h1><%= @product.name %></h1></li>
        <li> <div style="width:100%; vertical-align: middle; text-align: center">
          <% if !blank(product.photo) %>
              <img style='height:54px' src='<%= product.photo %>'>
            <% else %>
              <img style='height:54px' src='/../public/images/custom/notfound.jpg'>
            <% end %>
        <li>Cost <%= @product.standardcost %> </li>
        <li>List Price <%= @product.listprice %> </li>
        <li>Tax <%= @product.tax %></li>
        <li>Shipping <%= @product.shipping %> </li>
    </ul>
  </div>
</div>
```

    iii. Save and close the file.

7. Debug using the AdventureWorks 2.3.3 profile in the application simulator.
   a. Close any files that remain open.
   b. Once the simulator is open, navigate to 'Main', 'Settings'.
      i. Select 'Reset Database', then **[Confirm]**.

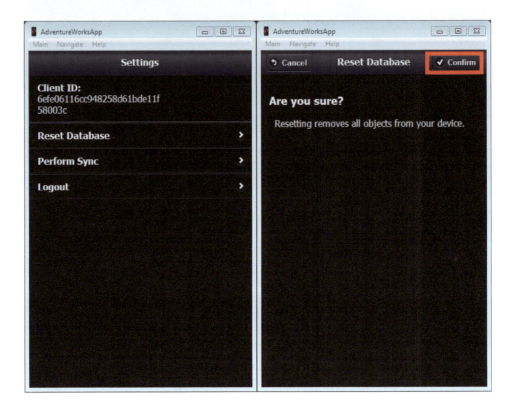

c. Once the application has completed synchronizing, navigate to 'Products', 'Clothing', 'Jerseys'. The following screen should be displayed.

d. Close the application simulator and all open files.

Exercise 4: Retrieve a Customer's Order History and Details

The end user may have to answer specific questions about a customer's previous order(s). This exercise brings orders and order details into the mobile application.

1. Create Source Adapters to retrieve order information via the web service.
    a. First, create the *Order* source adapter. Be sure the proper file is created in the /spec/ directory as well, and add the adapter to the **settings.yml** file.
        i. Open **AdventureWorksProvider\sources\order.rb**.
        ii. Add the login and query functions to the existing code.

```ruby
class Order < SourceAdapter
  def initialize(source)
    super(source)
  end

  def login
    raise SourceAdapterLoginException.new("1000") if !is_token_valid?
  end

  def query(params=nil)
    @result = {}
    # Query the web service
    orders = call_service("GetOrders")
    if !orders["Order"].nil?
      orders["Order"].each do |o|
        order = {}
        order["customerid"] = get(o,'CustomerID')
        order["dateordered"] = get(o,'DateOrdered')
        order["dateorderedraw"] = get(o,'DateOrderedRaw')
        order["dateshipmentdue"] = get(o,'DateShipmentDue')
        order["dateshipmentdueraw"] = get(o,'DateShipmentDueRaw')
        order["dateshipped"] = get(o,'DateShipped')
        order["dateshippedraw"] = get(o,'DateShippedRaw')
        order["orderid"] = get(o,'OrderID')
        order["ordernumber"] = get(o,'OrderNumber')
        order["purchaseordernumber"] = get(o,'PurchaseOrderNumber')
        order["shipping"] = get(o,'Shipping')
        order["shippingraw"] = get(o,'ShippingRaw')
        order["subtotal"] = get(o,'SubTotal')
        order["subtotalraw"] = get(o,'SubTotalRaw')
        order["taxamount"] = get(o,'TaxAmount')
        order["taxamountraw"] = get(o,'TaxAmountRaw')
        order["totaldue"] = get(o,'TotalDue')
        order["totaldueraw"] = get(o,'TotalDueRaw')

        # Set the value that is returned
        @result[order["orderid"]] = order
      end
    end
  end

  def sync
```

```
      # Manipulate @result before it is saved, or save it
      # yourself using the Rhoconnect::Store interface.
      # By default, super is called below which simply saves @result
      super
  end
end
```

iii. Save and close the file.

b. Create an *OrderDetail* source adapter. Be sure the proper file is created in the /spec/ directory as well, and add the adapter to the **settings.yml** file.

    i. Open **AdventureWorksProvider\sources\order_detail.rb.**

    ii. Add the login and query functions to the existing code.

```
class OrderDetail < SourceAdapter
  def initialize(source)
    super(source)
  end

  def login
    raise SourceAdapterLoginException.new("1000") if !is_token_valid?
  end

  def query(params=nil)
    @result = {}
    # Query the web service
    details = call_service("GetOrderDetails")
    if !details["OrderDetail"].nil?
      details["OrderDetail"].each do |od|
        detail = {}
        detail["discount"] = get(od,'Discount')
        detail["discountpercentage"] = get(od,'DiscountPercentage')
        detail["linetotal"] = get(od,'LineTotal')
        detail["linetotalraw"] = get(od,'LineTotalRaw')
        detail["orderdetailid"] = get(od,'OrderDetailID')
        detail["orderid"] = get(od,'OrderID')
        detail["productid"] = get(od,'ProductID')
        detail["quantity"] = get(od,'Quantity')
        detail["unitprice"] = get(od,'UnitPrice')
        detail["unitpriceraw"] = get(od,'UnitPriceRaw')

        # Set the value that is returned
        @result[detail["orderdetailid"]] = detail
      end
    end
  end

  def sync
    # Manipulate @result before it is saved, or save it
    # yourself using the Rhoconnect::Store interface.
    # By default, super is called below which simply saves @result
    super
  end
end
```

iii.   Save and close the file.

2. Create the *Order* and *OrderDetail* models in the mobile application using the Model Wizard.
Review Module 1, page 11 for details on creating the necessary models.

3. Activate synchronization.

   a.   Enable in the model.

   i.   Open **AdventureWorksApp\app\Order\order.rb**.

   ii.   Uncomment line 7.

```
6    # Uncomment the following line to enable sync with Order.
7    enable :sync
```

   iii.   Repeat step (ii) in **AdventureWorksApp\app\OrderDetail\order_detail.rb**.
   Note how Rhodes modified the file based on capitalization used in creating the model.

4. Orders will be available via two methods. An *Orders* item will be added to the main menu. An *Orders* element will also be added to the individual customer page, allowing quick access to a customer's order history.

   a.   Adding the Order as part of the Main Menu:

   i.   Begin by adding a list item pointing to the Order index page to
   AdventureWorksApp\index.erb.

```
<li><a href="<%= url_for(:controller => :Order, :action => :index) %>">Orders</a></li>
```

   ii.   Edit **AdventureWorksApp\app\Order\index.erb**.

      a.   Edit the header and remove the **[New]** button.

      b.   Create a listview containing the customer name, order number, order date, and total due. If the order has shipped, include a shipped date.
      Note the call to the Customer model to retrieve information for each order.

```
<div data-role="content">
  <ul data-role="listview">
    <% @orders.each do |order| %>
      <li>
        <a href="<%= url_for :action => :show, :id => order.object %>">
          <% @customer = Customer.find(order.customerid) %>
            <h3><%= @customer.companyname %></h3>
            <p> Amount: <%= order.totaldue %> | Order Date: <%= order.dateordered %><br/>
            <% if !blank?(order.dateshipped) %>
              Shipped:  <%= order.dateshipped %>
            <% else %>Shipment Pending
            <% end %></p>
        </a>
      </li>
    <% end %>
  </ul>
</div>
```

c. Test the application
   i. Save and close the file. Stop RhoConnect / Redis, and restart.
   ii. Run the application from the Debugging drop-down menu.
   iii. The following screen should be displayed once the *Orders* item is selected from the main menu.

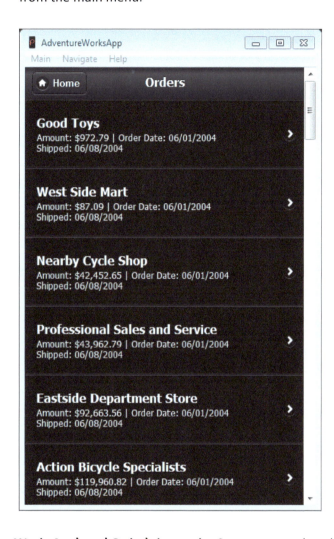

iii. Edit **AdventureWorksApp\app\Order\show.erb.** Create a page that shows specific order information, and a button linking to the order's details.
   a. The header is created automatically as part of the model wizard:

```
<div data-role="header" data-position="inline">
  <h1><%= @order.a %></h1>
    <a href="<%= url_for :action => :index %>" class="ui-btn-left" data-
icon="arrow-l" data-direction="reverse">
      Back
    </a>
    <a href="<%= url_for :action => :edit, :id => @style.object %>" class="ui-
btn-right" data-icon="star">
      Edit
    </a>
</div>
```

b. Edit the header.
  i. Change the heading from a variable to the static text "Order Info".
  ii. Remove the **[Edit]** button.

```
<div data-role="header" data-position="inline">
  <h1>Order Info</h1>
    <a href="<%= url_for :action => :index %>" class="ui-btn-left" data-icon="arrow-l"
data-direction="reverse">
      Back
    </a>
</div>
```

c. Within the content div, create a simple item list view for the Order information. Note how the customer information is obtained from the Customer model.

```
<div data-role="content">
  <ul data-role="listview">
    <% @customer = Customer.find(@order.customerid) %>
      <li> <%= @customer.companyname %>
      <li>Order ID:   <%= @order.orderid %> </li>
      <li>Order Number: <%= @order.ordernumber  %> </li>
      <li>Customer PO No.: <%= @order.purchaseordernumber  %> </li>
      <li>Ordered:  <%= @order.dateordered  %> </li>
      <li>Due:   <%= @order.dateshipmentdue  %> </li>
      <li>Shipped: <%= @order.dateshipped  %> </li>
      <li>Subtotal: <%= @order.subtotal  %> </li>
      <li>Shipping: <%= @order.shipping  %> </li>
      <li>Tax: <%= @order.taxamount  %> </li>
      <li>Total Due: <%= @order.totaldue  %> </li>
  </ul>
<div>
```

d. Create a button in the content div linking to details of the specific order. The new method *show_order* (created in the next step) is used to display a listing of all Order Details associated with an *orderid*. Note that the *orderid* is passed as the object's ID.

```
  <br/>
    <a href="<%= url_for(:controller => :OrderDetail, :action => :show_order, :query =>
{:id => @order.orderid}) %>" data-role="button" data-mini="true">Order Details</a>
```

e. Save and close the file.

iv.   Edit **AdventureWorksApp\app\OrderDetail\order_detail_controller.rb**.

   a.   Create the *show_order* method. This method finds all order details associated with the *orderid* passed from the button created on the **AdventureWorksApp\app\order\show.erb** page.

```ruby
def show_order
  @details = OrderDetail.find(
    :all,
    :order => ['orderdetailid'],
    :orderdir => ['ASC'],
    :conditions => {
      {
        :name=>'orderid',
        :op=>'='
      } => @params['id']
    }
  )
  render :action => :index
end
```

   b.   Save and close the file.

v.   Edit **AdventureWorksApp\app\OrderDetail\index.erb**.

   a.   Write code for the content div.

```erb
<div data-role="content">
    <ul data-role="listview">
      <% @details.each do |detail| %>
        <% @product = Product.find(detail.productid) %>
          <li>
            <a href="<%= url_for(:controller => :Product, :action => :show, :id =>
detail.productid) %>">
              <h3><%= @product.name %></h3>
              Qty: <%= detail.quantity %> | Disc: <%= detail.discountpercentage %> |
Total: <%= detail.linetotal %>
            </a>
          </li>
      <% end %>
    </ul>
  </div>
```

   b.   Save and close the file.

vi. Run the application using the Debugging drop-down menu.

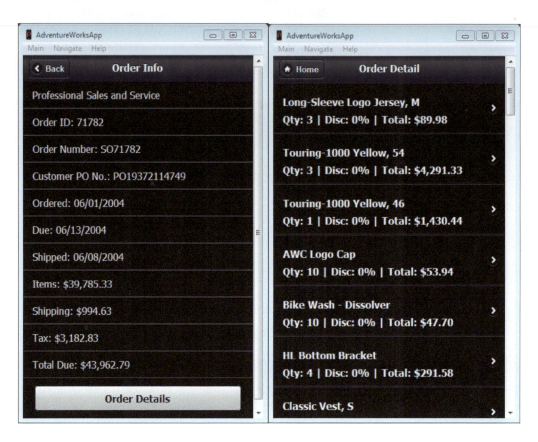

b. The second method for viewing orders from the customer view. Add a button allowing the user to open a list of orders for the current customer.

      i. Open **AdventureWorksApp\app\order\order_controller.rb.**

          a. Create the *by_customer* method. This method filters orders based on the *:id* parameter that is passed through the button on the customer page. Note that the list is sorted in descending order based on the *dateorderedraw* variable.

```ruby
def by_customer
  @orders = Order.find(
    :all,
    :order => ['dateorderedraw'],
    :orderdir => ['DESC'],
    :conditions => {
      {
      :name=>'customerid',
      :op=>'='
      } => @params['id']
    }
  )
  render :action => :index
end
```

          b. Save and close the file.

ii.   Open **AdventureWorksApp\app\Customer\show.erb.**

    a. Create a button within the content div but below list items. The button will link to the new method created in the *Order* controller, displaying only orders associated with the specific customer.

```
<div>
  <br/>

    <a href="<%= url_for(:controller => :Order, :action => :by_customer, :query => {:id
=> @customer.customerid}) %>" data-role="button">Order Details</a>

</div>
```

    b. Save and close the file.

iii.   Run the application using the Debugging drop-down menu.

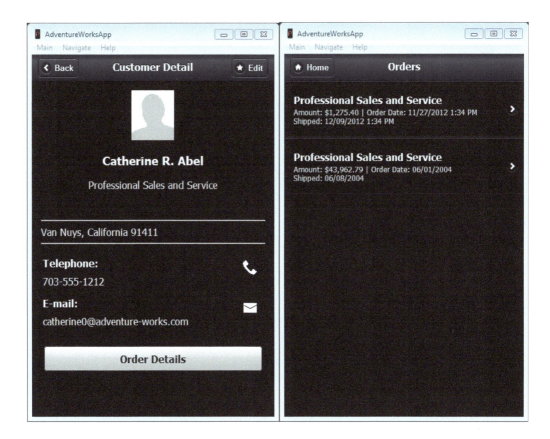

Exercise 5: Sell a Product

The application user may need to perform a simple order for a customer. In this exercise, the order will begin on a specific product's page. A link from the product page will start the order process, carrying the product information to a customer selection page. Once a customer is selected, the product and customer information is passed to the order page.

1. Open **AdventureWorksApp\app\product\show.erb.**
    a. Create a **[Sell]** button in the header of the product *show.erb* page.
       Parameters from the page are passed using the *:query* method.

```
<div data-role="header" data-position="inline">
    <h1>Product Details</h1>
    <a href="<%= url_for :action => :index %>" class="ui-btn-left" data-icon="arrow-l" data-
direction="reverse">
       Back
    </a>

    <a href="<%= url_for(:controller => :Customer, :action => :select_customer, :query => {:product
=> @product.productid, :product_name => @product.name})%>" class="ui-btn-right" data-icon="star">
       Sell
    </a>
  </div>
```

    b. Save and close the file.

2. Open **AdventureWorksApp\app\customer\customer_controller.rb.**
    a. Add the *:select_customer* method.
    b. Display a customer list, so that the user can select the ordering customer.
        i. OPTION 1: Return a single, non-paginated list of all customers. The user can filter the list using a text box at the top of the page. This list takes time to load.

```
def select_customer
  @customers =Customer.find(:all, :order => 'lastname') do |x,y|
    x.downcase <=> y.downcase
  end
  render :action => :select_customer
end
```

        ii. OPTION 2 (Recommended): Return a list of the first 60 customers only, for development and testing purposes.

```
def select_customer
  @customers =Customer.paginate(:page => 0, :per_page => 60, :order => 'lastname') do |x,y|
    x.downcase <=> y.downcase
  end
  render :action => :select_customer
end
```

3. Create the file **AdventureWorksApp\app\customer\select_customer.erb.**
   This is the view to that allows the user to select the ordering customer. The product ID and name, along with the customer ID and name, are passed forward to the *Order* controller upon the user's selection.
   A product cannot be sold to a customer without a shipping address, so display "Mobile Sales Not Available" to those customers without a shipping address.

```
<div data-role="page">
  <div data-role="header" data-position="inline">
    <h1>Select Customer</h1>
      <a href="<%= Rho::RhoConfig.start_path %>" class="ui-btn-left" data-icon="home" data-
direction="reverse" <%= "data-ajax='false'" if is_bb6 %>>
      Home
      </a>
  </div>

  <div data-role="content">
    <ul data-role="listview" data-filter="true">
      <% @customers.each do |customer| %>
        <li>
          <% if !blank?(customer.addressline1) %>
            <a href="<%= url_for(:controller => :Order, :action => :order, :query => {:customer
=> customer.customerid, :customer_name => customer.companyname, :product => @params['product'],
:product_name => @params['product_name']})%>">
              <% if !blank?(customer.photo) %>
                <img style='height:54px, vertical-alignment:middle' src='<%= customer.photo %>'>
              <% else %>
                <img style='height:54px' src='/../public/images/custom/portrait.gif'>
              <% end %>
              <%= customer.lastname %>, <%= customer.firstname %> <%= customer.middlename %><br/>
                <% if !blank?(customer.companyname) %>
                  <%= customer.companyname %>
                <% end %>
            </a>
          <% else %>
            <% if !blank?(customer.photo) %>
              <img style='height:54px, vertical-alignment:middle' src='<%= customer.photo %>'>
            <% else %>
              <img style='height:54px' src='/../public/images/custom/portrait.gif'>
            <% end %>
            <%= customer.lastname %>, <%= customer.firstname %> <%= customer.middlename %><br/>
              <% if !blank?(customer.companyname) %>
                <%= customer.companyname %>
              <% end %>
            <br/>
            <b>Mobile Sales Not Available</b>
          <% end %>
        </li>
      <% end %>
    </ul>
  </div>
</div>
```

a. Save and close the file.

4. Update **AdventureWorksApp\app\order\order_controller.rb**.

    a. Add the *order* method. When the method is called, the user is directed to the **new.erb** page.

```
def order
  @order = Order.new
  render :action => :new
end
```

    b. Add the *format_currency* method.

```
def format_currency( value, pre_symbol='$', thousands=',' )
    "#{pre_symbol}#{
      ( "%.2f" % value ).gsub(
        /(\d)(?=(?:\d{3})+(?:$|\.))/,
        \\1#{thousands}
      )
    }"
  end
```

    c. Update the *create* method. Unlike the update method used for the customer's telephone number, an entire order is being added to the table. The order information will not be available until the next synchronization, therefore the information from the order form must be stored locally so that it displays on the order list.

```
def create
  order = Order.create(@params['order'])
  product = Product.find(@params['order']['product'])
  quantity = @params['order']['quantity'].to_i
  discount_percent = @params['order']['discountPercent'].to_i
  customer = @params['order']['customer'].to_i

  # Information won't be retrieved from the server until the next sync
  # Populate what we can so we can display some information
  order.orderid = order.object # Temporary ID
  order.customerid = customer
  order.purchaseordernumber = @params['order']['purchaseordernumber']
  order.dateordered = "#{Time.new.strftime("%m/%d/%Y")}"
  order.dateshipmentdue = ""
  order.dateshipped = ""

  # Calculate what the order will return
  order.subtotalraw = quantity * product.listpriceraw.to_i * ((100 - discount_percent) / 100)
  order.shippingraw = order.subtotalraw * 0.025
  order.taxamountraw = order.subtotalraw * 0.08
  order.totaldueraw = order.subtotalraw + order.shippingraw + order.taxamountraw

  # Format it for display
  order.subtotal = format_currency(order.subtotalraw)
  order.shipping = format_currency(order.shippingraw)
  order.taxamount = format_currency(order.taxamountraw)
```

```
      order.totaldue = format_currency(order.totaldueraw)

      order.save
      redirect :action => :index

    end
```

d. Save and close the file.

5. Write the code for **AdventureWorksApp\app\order\new.erb.**
    This will be the input form. The Customer ID and Product ID are brought forward from the user's previous actions, and are placed in hidden input areas for pass-through to the web service call.

```
div data-role="page">
  <div data-role="header" data-position="inline">
    <h1>New Product Sale</h1>
    <a href="<%= url_for :action => :index %>" class="ui-btn-left" data-icon="back" data-
direction="reverse">
      Cancel
    </a>
  </div>

  <div data-role="content">
   <div>Sold To: <%= @params['customer_name'] %> <br/>
       Product: <%= @params['product_name'] %> </div>
         <br/>
         <br/>
    <form method="POST" action="<%= url_for :action => :create %>">
      <input type="hidden" id="order[product]" name="order[product]" value="<%= @params['product']
%>"/>
      <input type="hidden" id="order[customer]" name="order[customer]" value="<%=
@params['customer'] %>"/>

      <div data-role="fieldcontain">
        <label for="order[quantity]" class="fieldLabel">Quantity</label>
        <input type="text" id="order[quantity]" name="order[quantity]" <%= placeholder("1") %> />
      </div>

      <div data-role="fieldcontain">
        <label for="order[discount]" class="fieldLabel">Discount Percent</label>
        <input type="text" id="order[discount]" name="order[discount]" <%= placeholder("0") %> />
      </div>

      <div data-role="fieldcontain">
        <label for="order[purchaseordernumber]" class="fieldLabel">Purchase Order No.</label>
        <input type="text" id="order[purchaseordernumber]" name="order[purchaseordernumber]" <%=
placeholder("11-2222") %> />
      </div>

      <input type="submit" value="Create"/>
    </form>
  </div>
</div>
```

a. Save and close the file.

6. Update **AdventureWorksApp\order\index.rb**.

   a. The information on any order entered that has not synchronized with the enterprise data source will not have order details available. Write an *if-else* statement using `order.dateshipped` - a variable that remains empty until after synchronization.

```
<li>
  <% if blank?(order.dateshipped) %>
    <% @customer = Customer.find(order.customerid) %>
      <h3><%= @customer.companyname %> </h3>
      <p> Amount: <%= order.totaldue %> | Order Date: <%= order.dateordered %><br/>
      Additional Order Info Available Shortly
  <% else %>
    <a href="<%= url_for :action => :show, :id => order.object %>">
      <% @customer = Customer.find(order.customerid) %>
      <h3><%= @customer.companyname %> </h3>
      <p> Amount: <%= order.totaldue %> | Order Date: <%= order.dateordered %><br/>
      <% if !blank?(order.dateshipped) %>
        Shipped:   <%= order.dateshipped %>
      <% else %>Shipment Pending
      <% end %></p>
    </a>
  <%end %>
</li>
```

7. Update **AdventureWorksProvider\sources\order.rb**.

   a. Stop Redis and RhoConnect, using either the command line or batch file.

   b. Open **AdventureWorksProvider\sources\order.rb**.

```
def create(create_hash)
    c = create_hash
        if !c["product"].nil?
            val =
call_service("SellProduct","&customerID=#{c["customer"]}&productID=#{c["product"]}&quantity=#{c["qu
antity"]}&purchaseOrderNo=#{c["purchaseordernumber"]}&discountPercent=#{c["discount"]}")
            if !val["content"].start_with?("ERROR")
                items = val["content"].split("/")
                items.each do |item|
                  parts = item.split(":")
                    # Only interested in the OrderID
                    return parts[1].strip if parts[0] == "OrderID"
                end
            end
        end
end
```

   c. Save and close all open files.

8. Test the application.
   a. Stop and restart RhoConnect and Redis.
   b. Run the application using the Debugging drop-down menu.
   c. Navigate to a Product and select the **[Sell]** button.

d. Select a customer.

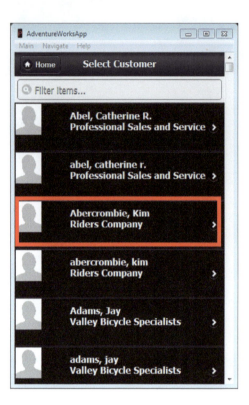

e. Fill in the order form. The Discount Percent should be an integer between 0- 100 and the Purchase Order No. must number. Select **[Create]**.

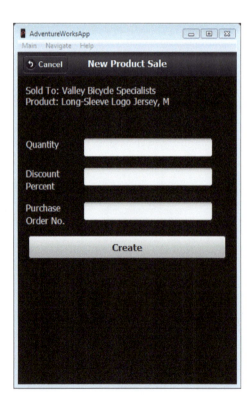

f. The once the order is created, the application should redirect to the order index page. The new order appears at the top of the list, and the user is unable to select the item.

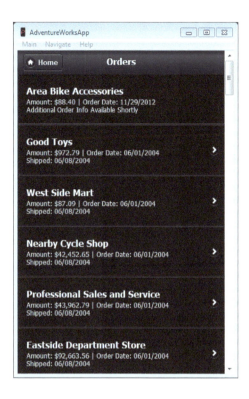

g. Once the application synchronizes with the server (3-5 minutes, dependent upon the application settings) and the order information is processed, the order and order details will be available.

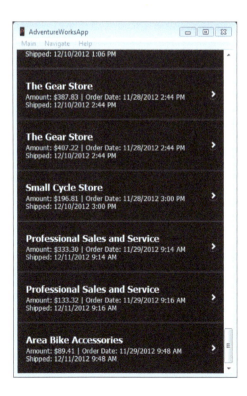

Congratulations!

This completes a sequence of 18 exercises designed to introduce mobile application development using RhoStudio. At this point, the application built will:

- Access Oak Tree Systems' modified enterprise data source
- Display company information about the "AdventureWorks" company, display a map of the location, and allow use of the phone's features to call and e-mail the company.
- Display a list of AdventureWorks customers, and allow use of the phone's features to call and e-mail each without having to have the information in the phone's contact manager.
- From the customer screen, display a list of orders for that specific customer.
- Edit any customer's phone number.
- Display a list of AdventureWorks products by category and sub-category.
- Display a list of all orders and order details.
- Create a simple product order.

These exercises are meant to give a developer a basic introduction to RhoMobile and mobile application development.

Working with RhoMobile

As with any development platform, there are a number of idiosyncrasies that new developers should be aware of.

General Notes on the Eclipse IDE

1. RhoMobile requires the folder structure that it creates to help it determine routing. Models cannot be reorganized so that controllers, models, etc. are together like a standard Rails application.

2. All of the files created by default with each Model may not be necessary.

   - If a model is only used to hold data and queried from other Models, then all that is needed is the Model file.
   - If a model simply transfers a user or displays information. It does not necessarily need a Model. It may only need a Controller and pages (or no pages depending on the scenario).
   - If there are no plans to develop for BlackBerry devices, delete all the BB files.
   - New, Edit, and Show files may not be necessary. If they are not, delete them and the corresponding code in the Controller to clean up the files.

3. The test files are not necessary to develop an application, but the tests can help locate issues.

4. In the Rhodes application, the top level index.erb file does not have a controller. If a controller is required in your top level index create the desired model, controller and start page. Set the start page location in application.rb.

5. Since the projects use Ruby, every Class is extendable. Custom functions can be added to any RhoMobile or default Ruby Class.

6. Use System.has_network() liberally. This default function checks to be sure the user has internet access through the mobile device. Good practice is to check the status before making a call that could potentially fail if the user does not have internet access.

7. Take full use of your exception backtraces to help quickly locate issues.
   ```ruby
   begin
     raise "Error" # An error!!!
     rescue Exception => e
     raise "Error Details: #{e.message}. Trace: #{e.backtrace}"
   end
   ```

8. It is not necessary to use hash tables for form input names on pages. This allows for more readable code in some cases. In other words, it is possible to do:
   ```ruby
   @model.attribute = @params['input_name']
   @model.save
   ```

   Rather than:
   ```ruby
   @model.update_attributes(@params['model'])
   ```

9. RhoMobile uses some code behind the scenes to make hashed models easier to work with. It is not necessary to refer to values by indexes like model[0] = index or model[1]["attribute"]. Instead, attributes can be referenced or updated with dot notation (e.g. model.attribute). There are a few exceptions to this rule when it comes to handling data in RhoConnect source adapters because the formatting code is not applied there.

10. RhoMobile within the Eclipse IDE auto-completes a significant amount of code. Depending on the habits of the developer, these auto-completions can be distracting or helpful. No preference is provided in the UI to change these settings. To reduce some of the code auto-completion, follow these steps:
    a. Close RhoMobile / Eclipse.
    b. Locate your workspace on your hard drive.
    c. Navigate to: .metadata\.plugins\org.eclipse.core.runtime\.settings

d. Open up org.eclipse.dltk.ruby.ui.prefs with a text editor
e. Add the following to the end:
    closeBrackets=false
    closeAngularBrackets=false
    closeBraces=false
    closeStrings=false

f. Save the file and close.
g. Reopen eclipse.

General Issues

Caching & History
Eclipse has a robust code history function. If a file is deleted, and later in the development cycle a file with the same name is created, old code will potentially be displayed in the file's contents. Eclipse loads the page from the local history. Close the file and reopen it. If the problem persists, replace the file content or delete the page and recreate it again.

Missing Files
Eclipse does not automatically refresh its content list. If files are added to the workspace projects outside of Eclipse, the file list in Eclipse needs to be right clicked on and then refreshed.

Out of Sync / Error when searching with Ctrl + H or Ctrl + F
Eclipse does not automatically refresh its content list. If files are changed outside of Eclipse, Eclipse does not know and may throw errors when trying to access the file contents. This is common with Rhodes because it updates files when it runs.

Unable to Create New Source Adapters
This is a known bug. After the first source adapter is created using the ***New, RhoConnect Source Adapter*** wizard, the wizard may cease to work. This issue appears to be related to Eclipse's history feature. There is no easy fix for the problem. Deleting and recreating the files / project sometimes resolves it, but there is no guarantee that it will work every time.

To work around the issue, copy and paste existing files. Remember to copy both the source and source_spec files. A prompt will allow you to rename the file when pasting it into the correct directory. Remember to edit settings.yml.

Using Source Control
Rhodes modifies files within the RhoMobile project when the project is run. If those files are read-only (which happens when using a 3rd party source control), Rhodes will not be able to make internal changes and will fail. Motorola recommends using Github™ for version control, but copying the project to a shared network folder is just as effective.

Rhoconnect Build Error: Could not Parse YAML in Settings.yml
Check the spacing of the items in the file. The parser is very specific about spacing. If items are not aligned and spaced properly, RhoConnect will not start successfully.

RhoConnect Delay: Changes Not Taking Effect

Occasionally, changes to RhoConnect are not propagated immediately. This is noticeable when the developer corrects an issue that was just identified. When this happens, it is necessary to stop and start RhoConnect and the Redis dependency again. Wait approximately 10 seconds between stopping and starting the RhoConnect instance to reduce the chances of this occurring.

Rhodes Application Error: Unknown Client

The RhoConnect server was likely reset, but not the Rhodes application. An old (unrecognized) ClientID may be in use.

Rhodes Application Error: Server returned an error

This error can occur if a syncing Model in the application cannot find a matching model in RhoConnect. Verify that the class name for the RhoConnect matching model is correct.

Rhodes Application Error: Data is not being updated

There are several reasons data may not be updated:

1. Sync is not enabled in the model.

2. The structure of the data changed significantly in the RhoConnect source adapter. This results in a mismatch between cached application data and new data sent from RhoConnect. Reset your application's database to resolve.

3. Your application is requesting data too quickly or too slowly. There are two settings that control data retrieval.
   - The application's polling interval specified at the Model level or in rhoconfig.txt in Rhodes. This setting affects how often the application requests data from RhoConnect.

   - The server polling interval is specified in RhoConnect's settings.yml. This setting affects how often RhoConnect will serve up data to applications requesting it. In other words, if the setting is 300 (the default), then RhoConnect will only give the application the latest copy of the information once every 5 minutes. Otherwise, RhoConnect tells the application to work with what it already has.

Rhodes Application: Sorting Returned Data

Data is sorted by case then alphabetically. In other words, it sorts using the character addresses instead of disregarding case. To keep records sorted correctly, block statements must be used.

Rhodes Application Navigation: Device Back Button Does Not Work Correctly

This often occurs because the ':back' option is specified for renders or redirects in the controller. For Android applications, this is not necessary because the application is running within a web server on the device. The phone automatically keeps track of the user's navigation history.

Rhodes Application Navigation: Navigation Does Not Work Correctly

There are a few reasons navigation can become problematic:

a. A data-url could have been specified on the page's topmost div that has a page role. This is used as a relative URL for all actions occurring from the page.

b. If the render, redirect, or Webview.Navigate all have correct routes specified, verify that they are the last action specified in the code because only the last request is processed. For example, if there is code that says to redirect, but it is followed by a render, only the render will be processed. Using an 'if' statement to separate the values so that only the correct action is set for the current situation resolves the issue.

c. Verify that the file names of your Models are correct if pages were copied and pasted then renamed. If the model is ProductCategory, the controller needs to be called product_category_controller.

d. The RhoMobile MVC model applies certain navigation behaviors to pages based on the page name. If the page is called "index.erb", the navigation treats it as a top level page. If the page is called something else, the page expects an "id" parameter which it adds as a subdirectory to the request.

RhoSimulator: Log Display Issues

This issue appears to occur if the log window is dragged outside the boundaries of the monitor area. To view the log information after it has this issue, maximize the log. Eventually, after several runs, the window will be restored to the full dimensions of the monitor and can be resized down.

Appendix A: Developer Installation

Working With RhoMobile for Windows

This installation document covers **RhoConnect 3.2.0** and **Rhodes 3.3.3** which are installed with **RhoMobile 2.0.5**. All batch files can be found on Oak Tree's RhoMobile Dropbox site in the *Developer Batch Files & Information* directory.

Ruby Installation

Ruby 1.9.3 is required. **Version p125** is recommended because newer versions cause an error in the eventmachine gem that is used by the version of the thin gem that RhoConnect runs under which prevents it from running.

Issue: https://github.com/eventmachine/eventmachine/issues/319

Ruby Installer Download URL: http://rubyinstaller.org/downloads/

Installation Steps

During the install, check the following options:

- Add Ruby executables to your PATH
- Associate .rb and .rbw files with this Ruby installation

RhoMobile Installation

Go to http://www.motorola.com/Business/US-EN/RhoMobile%20Suite/Downloads.

Download current installation file from Motorola's RhoMobile website.

This installation will install the **Rhodes** framework and **RhoConnect** along with a custom **Eclipse** installation. A default set of ruby gems will also be installed. Additional versions of the gems may be installed as part of the initial setup process.

Install Gems

Additional Gems, self-contained ruby code, may need to be installed so that RhoConnect projects that are created can be run. If RhoConnect does not function, create the 'Developer Installer.bat' file from the code in this appendix or download from Oak Tree's RhoMobile Dropbox site. Use the batch file to install a known working configuration of gems. The project's gemlist files may also need to be updated to match the supplied versions.

Before starting the install, right click on the batch file and choose edit. Verify that the paths specified at the top of the file are accurate.

1. Open "Developer Installer.bat"
2. Make sure gems.txt is in the same directory as the batch file.
3. Choose: "Start Install"

RhoConnect

RhoConnect is used to query data sources for information and serve the information up to mobile applications. If RhoConnect is not running, applications cannot retrieve any information to display.

The current version of RhoConnect uses Redis, an in-memory (stored in RAM) database server, to store results. Redis stores the information using name-value pairs.

RhoConnect is launched and managed using command line tools. To make this process easier, code for a batch file called "Developer RhoMobile.bat" is provided. The file can be created from code in this appendix or downloaded from Oak Tree's RhoMobile Dropbox site.

Before using the batch file for the first time, right click on the batch file and choose edit. Verify that the paths specified at the top of the file are accurate. Additionally, make sure you set your RhoConnect project name in the file.

Create a Developer Batch file for each project, storing it in the application workspace. This avoids constantly changing the project name.

Developer RhoMobile.bat Options

1. **Start RhoConnect server**

    This option will launch Redis then RhoConnect. The Redis window should show a client connection when RhoConnect has finished initializing. RhoConnect will say it is listening on a specific port.

    If the RhoConnect window disappears, try starting it with the build errors option to see if there is a typo in the code. If it launches, but does not connect to Redis, verify that the gem configuration is correct.

2. **Stop RhoConnect server and exit**

    This option is used to close both RhoConnect and Redis in that order. This is necessary so that temporary files are deleted or created by the processes.

3. **Open RhoConnect admin console**

    This option can be used to view data associated with user accounts, remove device access, or view server response time statistics.

4. **Open Command Prompt with Ruby**

    This option can be used if additional command line options need to be run.

5. **Build Android APK**

    This option can be used to build a deployable Android APK file for phones. Both the Android NDK and SDK as well as an acceptable version of the Java JDK (1.6.0 as of this writing) need to be installed and the paths need to be set in the RhoMobile Eclipse Preferences.

6. **Start RhoConnect only for Build Errors**

    If the RhoConnect CMD window disappears when the Start option is chosen, it is likely that there is an issue with the code in the project. Use this option to launch the project without the exit flag so the window stays open. Then, if an error is thrown, it can be read.

Appendix A: Developer Installation

Create Developer Installer.bat

This installer file creates a known working configuration of GEMS. This file may also be downloaded from Oak Tree's RhoMobile Dropbox site.

```
@echo off
REM Type 'help color' in a command window to view color options
color 1B
(title Developer Installer)

REM Update the value with your RhoMobileSuite path
(set rhoSuitePath=C:\Motorola\RhoMobileSuite)

REM Update the path to your Command Prompt with Ruby
REM To locate, right click on the Command Prompt with Ruby link in the Ruby installation on the Start Menu
REM Choose Properties and copy the path from the target
(set rubyCmd=C:\Ruby193\bin\setrbvars.bat)

REM Present options to the user
:start
echo Running scripts from:
echo %rhoSuitePath%
echo.
echo Update batch file if this is not correct.
echo.
echo    0 - Exit
echo    1 - Start gem install (up to hour)
echo    3 - List gems
REM echo    5 - Uninstall all gems
echo.

REM Prompt for a selection and handle it
set /p choice="Enter your choice: "
if "%choice%"=="0" exit
if "%choice%"=="1" goto :doinstall
if "%choice%"=="3" goto :gems
REM if "%choice%"=="5" goto :douninstall
echo Invalid choice: %choice%
echo.
pause
cls
goto :start

REM Install gems that are known to work
:doinstall
cls
echo Installing the required gems...
echo This will take several minutes...
echo.
echo Copying gem list to installation directory...
xcopy gems.txt %rhoSuitePath%
echo.
echo Moving to specified RhoSuite directory...
cd %rhoSuitePath%
echo.
echo Validating file copy...
if exist gems.txt (
    echo Copy Successful
) else (
    echo Copy Failed
)
echo.
```

```
echo Installing gems to RhoSuite for Rhodes...
echo Starting at %TIME%
FOR /F "delims=;" %%G  IN (gems.txt) DO (
    echo Queued: %%G
    START /wait CMD /E:ON /K cd %rhoSuitePath% ^& gem install %%G ^& exit
)
echo.
echo Ending at %TIME%
echo.
echo Installing gems to Ruby for RhoConnect...
echo Starting at %TIME%
FOR /F "delims=;" %%G  IN (gems.txt) DO (
    echo Queued: %%G
    START /wait CMD /E:ON /K %rubyCmd% ^& cd %rhoSuitePath% ^& gem install %%G ^& exit
)
echo.
echo Ending at %TIME%
echo.
echo Removing gem list...
DEL gems.txt
echo.
echo Validating file copy...
if exist gems.txt (
    echo Delete Failed
) else (
    echo Delete Successful
)
echo.
goto :start

REM List installed gems
:gems
cls
echo Displaying RhoSuite current gems...
START CMD /E:ON /K cd %rhoSuitePath% ^& echo RhoSuite gems: ^& gem list
echo Displaying Ruby current gems...
START CMD /E:ON /K %rubyCmd% ^& cd %rhoSuitePath% ^& echo Ruby gems: ^& gem list
goto :start

REM Load a Command Prompt window with Ruby, move to the applicable directory, and run the appropriate
commands
:douninstall
cls
echo Uninstalling all of your current gems from the ruby install...
REMSTART CMD /E:ON /K %rubyCmd% ^& cd %rhoSuitePath% ^& gem list ^| cut -d^" ^" -f1 ^| xargs gem uninstall -
aIx
echo Uninstalling all of your current gems from the RhoSuite install...
echo This will uninstall RhoElements which doesn't have a gem to install again.
REM START powershell.exe -noexit -command "gem list | %{$_.split(' ')[0]} | %{gem uninstall -Iax $_ }"
echo.
echo.
goto :start
```

Create Developer RhoMobile.bat

This file may also be downloaded from Oak Tree's RhoMobile Dropbox site.

```
@ECHO off
REM Type 'help color' in a command window to view color options
color 1B
(title Developer RhoMobile)

REM Update the value with your Rhodes workspace path
(set rhoAppPath=C:\Rho\workspace)

REM Update the value with your RhoConnect project
(set rhoConnectProject=TrainingForceStudentProvider)

REM Update the path to your Command Prompt with Ruby
REM To locate, right click on the Command Prompt with Ruby link in the Ruby installation on the Start Menu
REM Choose Properties and copy the path from the target
(set rubyCmd=C:\Ruby193\bin\setrbvars.bat)

REM Present options to the user
:start
  ECHO Some options may take up to 1-2 minutes to complete.
  ECHO.
  ECHO    0 - Exit
  ECHO    1 - Start RhoConnect server
  ECHO    2 - Stop RhoConnect server and exit
  ECHO    4 - Open RhoConnect admin console
  ECHO    5 - Open Command Prompt with Ruby
  ECHO    7 - Build Android APK
  ECHO    8 - Start RhoConnect only for Build Errors
  ECHO.

  REM Prompt for a selection and handle it
  set /p choice="Enter your choice: "
    if "%choice%"=="0" exit
    if "%choice%"=="1" goto startserver
    if "%choice%"=="2" goto stopserver
    if "%choice%"=="4" goto openconsole
    if "%choice%"=="5" goto openprompt
    if "%choice%"=="7" goto buildapk
    if "%choice%"=="8" goto startonlyrho
  ECHO Invalid choice: %choice%
  ECHO.
  pause
  CLS
goto start

REM Load a Command Prompt window with Ruby, move to the applicable directory, and run the appropriate
commands
:startserver
  CLS
  ECHO Starting the RhoConnect server:
  ECHO.
  ECHO    Starting Redis then...
    REM Exit command window after doing command because it launches in a new window
    START /MIN CMD /E:ON /K %rubyCmd% ^
              ^& cd %rhoAppPath%\%rhoConnectProject% ^
              ^& rhoconnect redis-start ^
              ^& exit

  ECHO    Starting RhoConnect...
    START /MIN CMD /E:ON /K %rubyCmd% ^
```

```
                ^& cd %rhoAppPath%\%rhoConnectProject% ^
                ^& rhoconnect start ^
                ^& exit

    ECHO.
    ECHO.
goto start

REM Load a Command Prompt window with Ruby, move to the applicable directory, and run the appropriate
commands
:openconsole
    CLS
    ECHO Opening the RhoConnect admin console...
    ECHO If the browser page does not load, RhoConnect has not finished starting yet.
    ECHO Try refreshing the browser page if that is the case or check for errors.
        START /MIN CMD /E:ON /K %rubyCmd% ^
                ^& cd %rhoAppPath%\%rhoConnectProject% ^
                ^& rhoconnect web ^
                ^& exit

    ECHO.
    ECHO.
goto start

REM Load a Command Prompt window with Ruby, move to the applicable directory
:openprompt
    CLS
    ECHO Opening a Command Prompt with Ruby...
        START CMD /E:ON /K %rubyCmd% ^
            ^& cd %rhoAppPath%\%rhoConnectProject%
    ECHO.
    ECHO.
goto start

REM Load a Command Prompt window with Ruby, move to the applicable directory, and run the appropriate
commands
:stopserver
    CLS
    ECHO Stopping the RhoConnect server:
    ECHO     Stopping RhoConnect then...
        START /MIN CMD /E:ON /K %rubyCmd% ^
                ^& cd %rhoAppPath%\%rhoConnectProject% ^
                ^& rhoconnect stop ^
                ^& exit

    ECHO     Stopping Redis...
        START /MIN CMD /E:ON /K %rubyCmd% ^
                ^& cd %rhoAppPath%\%rhoConnectProject% ^
                ^& rhoconnect redis-stop ^
                ^& exit

exit

REM Load a Command Prompt window, move to the Rhodes app directory, build
:buildapk
    CLS
    set /p app="Project name in workspace: "
    ECHO APK location: %rhoAppPath%\%app%\bin\target\android\
    ECHO Starting APK build...
        START CMD /E:ON /K cd %rhoAppPath%\%app% ^
        ^& rake device:android:production

    ECHO.
```

```
  ECHO.
goto start

REM Load a Command Prompt window with Ruby, move to the applicable directory, and run the appropriate
commands
:startonlyrho
  CLS
  ECHO Starting the RhoConnect only:
  ECHO.
  ECHO     Starting RhoConnect...
    REM Remove ' ^& exit' from end if debugging to display build errors
    REM The command window closes immediately after encountering them otherwise
    START /MIN CMD /E:ON /K %rubyCmd% ^
              ^& cd %rhoAppPath%\%rhoConnectProject% ^
              ^& rhoconnect start

  ECHO.
  ECHO.
goto start
```

Create Gems.txt

This file may also be downloaded from Oak Tree's RhoMobile Dropbox site.

```
activesupport -v 2.3.14;
activesupport -v 3.2.3;
async-rack -v 0.5.1;
bigdecimal -v 1.1.0;
bundler -v 1.1.3;
daemon_controller -v 1.0.0;
daemons -v 1.1.8;
diff-lcs -v 1.1.3;
eventmachine -v 1.0.0.beta.4.1;
extlib -v 0.9.15;
fastthread -v 1.0.7;
highline -v 1.6.11;
highline -v 1.6.12;
i18n -v 0.6.0;
io-console -v 0.3;
json -v 1.5.4;
json -v 1.6.7;
macaddr -v 1.5.0;
macaddr -v 1.6.0;
mime-types -v 1.18;
minitest -v 2.5.1;
mspec -v 1.5.17;
multi_json -v 1.3.4;
multi_json -v 1.3.5;
multi_json -v 1.3.6;
nokogiri -v 1.5.2;
passenger -v 3.0.12;
rack -v 1.3.6;
rack -v 1.4.1;
rack-fiber_pool -v 0.9.2;
rack-protection -v 1.2.0;
rack-test -v 0.6.1;
rake -v 0.9.2.2;
rdoc -v 3.9.4;
redis -v 2.2.2;
redis-namespace -v 1.0.3;
resque -v 1.20.0;
```

```
resque -v 1.19.0;
rest-client -v 1.6.7;
rhoconnect -v 3.1.1;
rhoconnect -v 3.2.0;
rhoconnect-adapters -v 1.0.3;
rhodes -v 3.3.3;
rhodes-translator -v 0.0.4;
rhomobile-debug -v 1.0.6;
rspec -v 2.6.0;
rspec-core -v 2.6.4;
rspec-expectations -v 2.6.0;
rspec-mocks -v 2.6.0;
rubygems-update -v 1.8.21;
rubygems-update -v 1.8.24;
rubyzip -v 0.9.8;
setup -v 5.1.0;
sinatra -v 1.3.2;
sqlite3 -v 1.3.6;
systemu -v 2.2.0;
systemu -v 2.5.0;
templater -v 1.0.0;
thin -v 1.3.1;
thor -v 0.14.6;
tilt -v 1.3.3;
uuid -v 2.3.5;
uuidtools -v 2.1.1;
uuidtools -v 2.1.2;
vegas -v 0.1.11;
win32-api -v 1.4.8
win32-process -v 0.6.5;
windows-api -v 0.4.1;
windows-pr -v 1.2.1;
xml-simple -v 1.1.1;
```

Appendix A: Developer Installation

Appendix B: Windows 2003 Server Installation

This installation document covers **RhoConnect 3.2.0** which comes installed with **RhoMobile 2.0.5** to a Windows 2003 Server. All necessary installation files are located in Oak Tree Systems' Dropbox.

Ruby Installation

Ruby 1.9.3 is required. **Version p125** is recommended because newer versions cause an error in the eventmachine gem that is used by the version of the thin gem that RhoConnect runs under which prevents it from running.

Issue: https://github.com/eventmachine/eventmachine/issues/319

Ruby Installer Download URL: http://rubyinstaller.org/downloads/

Installation Steps

During the install, check the following options:
- Add Ruby executables to your PATH
- Associate .rb and .rbw files with this Ruby installation

DevKit Installation

DevKit is required so native ruby gems can be compiled and installed. Without this package installed, some gems required by RhoConnect cannot be installed.

DevKit can be downloaded from: http://rubyinstaller.org/downloads/

Installation Steps

1. Install to: C:\RhoTools\DevKit
2. Run the "Server Config.bat" file that came with the installation instructions.
3. Choose "Open Command Prompt with Ruby"
4. Type: "cd C:\RhoTools\DevKit"
5. Type: "ruby dk.rb init" to generate a **config.yml** file that points to the ruby installation on the computer.
6. Type: "ruby dk.rb install" to DevKit enhance your Ruby installation.

Redis Installation

1. Copy supplied "redis-2.4.0" folder from Oak Tree's RhoMobile Dropbox site.
2. Place in: "C:\RhoTools\"

Environment Variables

Environment Variables need to be added so RhoConnect and Redis can run.

1. Right click on My Computer
2. Select Properties
3. Choose Advanced tab
4. Click Environment Variables
5. Locate PATH Environment variable in System variables.
6. Click Edit.
7. Paste the following on the end of it: C:\RhoTools\DevKit\bin;C:\RhoTools\DevKit\mingw\bin;C:\RhoTools\redis-2.4.0;

8. Click OK to update.
9. Click New under System variables.
10. Set Variable name to: REDIS_HOME
11. Set Variable value to: C:\RhoTools\redis-2.4.0

Note: It is important to leave the semicolon off the end of the REDIS_HOME value.

RhoConnect Projects

1. Create this folder: C:/RhoConnect/
2. Copy your RhoConnect project(s) to the folder.

Modify Batch Files

If you chose to install in a different installation path, you will need to do the following:

1. Right click on "Server Config.bat"
2. Choose: Edit.
3. Update the path for the rhoAppPath variable if it is different than the default.
4. Update the path for the rubyCmd variable if it is different than the default.

If you do not plan on running RhoConnect under LocalHost, modify the rhoConnectURL as well. The port specified in ports.txt later will be appended to the URL. For example, if http://127.0.0.1 was specified, the fully qualified URL would be similar to http://127.0.0.1:9292/api/application .

Install Gems

Gems, self-contained ruby code, need to be installed so that RhoConnect can run. Up to this point, only the tools required to install the gems that are used by RhoConnect have been installed.

1. Open "Server Installer.bat". This file can be created from the appendix or downloaded from Oak Tree's RhoMobile Dropbox site.
2. Make sure gems.txt is in the same directory as the batch file.
3. Choose: "Start Install"

```
Server Gem Installer                                    _ □ ×
Installing the required gems...
This will take several minutes...

Installing gems to Ruby for RhoConnect...
Starting at 13:43:28.04
Queued: async-rack -v 0.5.1
Queued: bigdecimal -v 1.1.0
Queued: bundler -v 1.1.3
Queued: daemons -v 1.1.8
Queued: eventmachine -v 1.0.0.beta.4.1
Queued: highline -v 1.6.12
Queued: io-console -v 0.3
Queued: mime-types -v 1.18
Queued: minitest -v 2.5.1
Queued: rack-fiber_pool -v 0.9.2
Queued: rack-test -v 0.6.1
```

The gems required for a standard installation are installed in a configuration that is known to work. The process can take up to an hour in extreme cases, but in most cases it takes around 10 minutes.

Configure RhoConnect Projects

The current version of RhoConnect uses Redis, an in-memory (stored in RAM) database server, to store results from the data for which it queries so that it can serve that information up to the applications on mobile devices. Redis stores the information using name-value pairs.

Each instance of RhoConnect needs its own Redis instance.

1. Open "Server Config.bat". This file can be created from this appendix or downloaded from Oak Tree's RhoMobile Dropbox site.
2. Choose: "Set Active RhoConnect Instance"

At this point and later when it is launched, the RhoConnect instance will be updated with several files in the settings folder.

- ports.txt – This file controls what ports RhoConnect and Redis use. Each instance of RhoConnect and Redis must use different ports. If you update this file and you currently have your project selected, you will need to reselect it to update the ports before launching the instance for testing.
- redis.conf – This file is copied from the redis folder. It controls all of the settings that are applied to the Redis instance that is launched. Changing the ports in ports.txt will update the ports in this file. Other changes are preserved so that you can configure Redis server to meet your particular needs. To reset the redis.conf file, simply delete it, and it will be recopied when you next choose the active instance.
- settings.yml – This file is updated to match the ports contained in ports.txt so RhoConnect knows what it is connecting to.
- dump.rdb – This file is added to the folder by Redis. It is added and updated periodically while Redis runs and when the instance is stopped. It contains the current copy of the in memory Redis database. Redis uses it to populate itself when it launches and offload items in the database that are not queried for a lot.

- RhoConnect.pid – This file stores the ID assigned to the RhoConnect instance when it is started. It will be deleted when the instance is stopped.

3. Choose "Start RhoConnect server" to verify that the configuration and installation were successful. Two command windows should remain open.

Redis will note when RhoConnect attaches to it.

RhoConnect will be listening for requests when it has successfully started.

If the information displayed in the windows is similar to the screenshots, then everything is configured and installed correctly and the windows can be closed. If the RhoConnect window does not stay open, something is wrong, and it will need to be checked for build errors.

Appendix B: Server Installation

Running Projects as a Service

Once the projects have been configured, the "Server Services.bat" file can be used to automatically launch any project specified when the server starts and keep it running in the background.

Before using the batch file, the Windows Server 2003 Resource Kit will need to be installed if it is not installed already. It can be downloaded from the following URL or installed using the supplied rktools.exe file. It is recommended that the Resource Kit be installed to C:\ResouceKit, but other locations will work.

http://www.microsoft.com/en-us/download/details.aspx?id=17657

The batch file will need to be configured before being used as well. By default, it will look for the Resource Kit in C:\ResourceKit.

Once projects have been installed as services, they need to be configured to run under a specific account.

1. Choose Administrative Tools under the Start menu and select Services.
2. Find the appropriate services and right click on them. Installed services will start with the words Redis and RhoConnect.
3. Choose Properties to configure them.
4. Choose the Log On tab and specify the account under which the services should run.

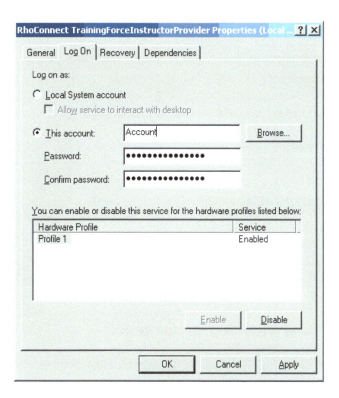

5. Choose the Recovery tab and specify any recovery options that may be relevant.

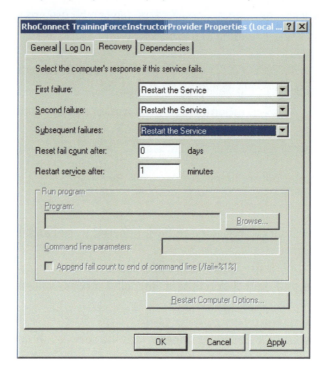

6. Finally, apply the changes and start the RhoConnect services. The RhoConnect services will automatically start the Redis service that they rely on.

If the project ports are changed, the service will need to be reinstalled.

Verify that Redis is running as a service:

1. Open up a command prompt.
2. Navigate to the Redis directory (by default, it is C:\RhoTools\redis-2.4.0).
3. Type "redis-cli –p <port configured with> ping" (e.g. redis-cli –p 6379 ping).

If Redis is running under the specified port, the response will be an immediate "PONG". If there is no immediate response, Redis is not running under the specified port or the command was typed incorrectly. Use Ctrl + Break to stop the request.

Verify that RhoConnect is running (takes several seconds after Redis):

Open up a browser window. Navigate to the URL to which RhoConnect was installed followed by a console subdirectory (e.g. 127.0.0.1:9292/console/). The RhoConnect console should be displayed. If no page loads, RhoConnect is not running or the URL was typed incorrectly.

Confirm and Open Ports

To allow mobile applications to connect to the RhoConnect instances, the ports specified for the RhoConnect projects to use must be opened up in any firewalls that restrict access to the server.

Create Server Installer.bat

This file may also be downloaded from [Oak Tree's RhoMobile Dropbox site.](#)

```
@echo off
REM Type 'help color' in a command window to view color options
color 1B
title Server Installer

REM Update the path to your Command Prompt with Ruby
REM To locate, right click on the Command Prompt with Ruby link in the Ruby installation on the Start Menu
REM Choose Properties and copy the path from the target
set rubyCmd=C:\Ruby193\bin\setrbvars.bat

REM Present options to the user
:start
echo Choose an option:
echo.
echo    0 - Exit
echo    1 - Start gem install (up to hour)
echo    3 - List gems
echo    5 - Uninstall all gems
echo.

REM Prompt for a selection and handle it
set /p choice="Enter your choice: "
if "%choice%"=="0" exit
if "%choice%"=="1" goto :doinstall
if "%choice%"=="3" goto :gems
if "%choice%"=="5" goto :douninstall
echo Invalid choice: %choice%
echo.
pause
cls
goto :start

REM Install gems that are known to work
:doinstall
cls
echo Installing the required gems...
echo This will take several minutes...
echo.
if exist gems.txt (
  echo Installing gems to Ruby for RhoConnect...
  echo Starting at %TIME%
  FOR /F "delims=;" %%G  IN (gems.txt) DO (
    echo Queued: %%G
    START /wait CMD /E:ON /K %rubyCmd% ^& gem install %%G ^& exit
  )
  echo.
  echo Ending at %TIME%
) else (
    echo INSTALL FAILED: Missing 'gems.txt'
)
echo.
goto :start

REM List installed gems
:gems
cls
echo Displaying Ruby current gems...
START CMD /E:ON /K %rubyCmd% ^& echo Ruby gems: ^& gem list
```

```
goto :start

REM Load a Command Prompt window with Ruby, move to the applicable directory, and run the appropriate
commands
:douninstall
cls
echo Uninstalling all of your current gems from the ruby install...
START CMD /E:ON /K %rubyCmd% ^& gem list ^| cut -d^" ^" -f1 ^| xargs gem uninstall -aIx
echo.
echo.
goto :start
```

Create Gems.txt

This file may also be downloaded from <u>Oak Tree's RhoMobile Dropbox site.</u>

```
async-rack -v 0.5.1;
bigdecimal -v 1.1.0;
bundler -v 1.1.3;
daemons -v 1.1.8;
eventmachine -v 1.0.0.beta.4.1;
highline -v 1.6.12;
io-console -v 0.3;
mime-types -v 1.18;
minitest -v 2.5.1;
rack-fiber_pool -v 0.9.2;
rack-test -v 0.6.1;
rdoc -v 3.9.4;
rspec -v 2.6.0;
rspec-core -v 2.6.4;
rspec-expectations -v 2.6.0;
rspec-mocks -v 2.6.0;
rhoconnect -v 3.2.0;
rhomobile-debug -v 1.0.6;
rubygems-update -v 1.8.24;
rubyzip -v 0.9.8;
sinatra -v 1.3.2;
sqlite3 -v 1.3.6;
thin -v 1.3.1;
uuidtools -v 2.1.1;
win32-process -v 0.6.5;
windows-api -v 0.4.1;
windows-pr -v 1.2.1;
xml-simple -v 1.1.1;
```

Create Server Config.bat

This file may also be downloaded from Oak Tree's RhoMobile Dropbox site.

```
@ECHO off
REM Type 'help color' in a command window to view color options
color 1B
title Server Config

REM Update this value if you are not running RhoConnect under LocalHost
SET rhoConnectURL=http://127.0.0.1

REM Update the value with your Rhodes workspace path
REM Redis database dump is also stored in this directory
SET rhoAppPath=C:\RhoConnect

REM Update the path to your Command Prompt with Ruby
REM To locate, right click on the Command Prompt with Ruby link in the Ruby installation on the Start Menu
REM Choose Properties and copy the path from the target
SET rubyCmd=C:\Ruby193\bin\setrbvars.bat

SETlocal EnableDelayedExpansion

REM Set some variables that get set based on user actions
SET rhoConnectProject=Default
set rhoConnectPort=Default
set redisPort=Default
set projPath=Default

REM Present options to the user
:start
  ECHO Some options may take up to 1-2 minutes to complete.
  ECHO.
  if NOT !rhoConnectProject!==Default (
    ECHO ACTIVE SERVER: !rhoConnectProject!
    ECHO.
  )
  ECHO    0 - Exit
  ECHO    1 - Set Active RhoConnect Instance
  if NOT !rhoConnectProject!==Default (
    ECHO    3 - Start RhoConnect server
    ECHO    4 - Stop RhoConnect server
    ECHO    5 - Open RhoConnect admin console
    ECHO    6 - Start RhoConnect only for Build Errors
  )
  ECHO    9 - Open Command Prompt with Ruby
  ECHO.

  REM Prompt for a selection and handle it
  SET /p choice="Enter your choice: "
    if "%choice%"=="0" exit
    if "%choice%"=="1" GOTO activeserver
    if "%choice%"=="3" GOTO startserver
    if "%choice%"=="4" GOTO stopserver
    if "%choice%"=="5" GOTO openconsole
    if "%choice%"=="6" GOTO startonlyrho
    if "%choice%"=="9" GOTO openprompt
  ECHO Invalid choice: %choice%
  ECHO.
  PAUSE
  cls
GOTO start
```

```
REM SET Server that user is working with
:activeserver
  cls

  REM First, count the instances
  SET total=0
  for /d %%X in (%rhoAppPath%\*) do SET /a total+=1

  if %total%==0 (
    ECHO No RhoConnect instances were found.
    ECHO Verify path in batch file and project locations.
  ) else (
    ECHO RhoConnect Instances:
    ECHO.

    REM List the available instances and present them for selection
    SET total=0
    for /d %%X in (%rhoAppPath%\*) do (
      SET /a total+=1
      SET instancePath=%%X
      SET instancePath=!instancePath:%rhoAppPath%\=!
      ECHO !total!. !instancePath!
    )
    ECHO.

    REM Have the user select an instance
    SET total=0
    SET /p instanceChoice="RhoConnect Instance: "
    SET instanceRequested="notrealfolder"

    for /d %%X in (%rhoAppPath%\*) do (
      SET /a total+=1
      if "!total!"=="!instanceChoice!" (
        SET instanceRequested=%%X
        REM Replace the Application Path with nothing so we just have the instance name
        SET instanceRequested=!instanceRequested:%rhoAppPath%\=!
      )
    )

    REM Locate the selection
    if exist %rhoAppPath%\!instanceRequested! (
      SET rhoConnectProject=!instanceRequested!
      SET projPath=%rhoAppPath%\!instanceRequested!

      ECHO.
      ECHO !instanceRequested!
      ECHO    Verifying configuration...

      REM Prep the instance if any files are missing
      CALL :prepports
      CALL :preprhoconnect
      CALL :prepredis

    ) else (
      ECHO    RhoConnect instance not found.
    )

  )
  ECHO.
GOTO start
```

```
REM Load a Command Prompt window with Ruby, move to the applicable directory, and run the appropriate
commands
:startserver
  cls
  ECHO Starting: !rhoConnectProject!

  if NOT exist !projPath!\settings\settings.yml (
    ECHO      settings.yml file missing in settings directory^^!
  ) else (
    ECHO      Starting Redis instance on port !redisPort!...
      REM Exit command window after doing command because it launches in a new window
      START /MIN CMD /E:ON /K %rubyCmd% ^
          ^& cd !projPath!\settings ^
          ^& title Redis - !rhoConnectProject! ^
          ^& %REDIS_HOME%\redis-server redis.conf ^
          ^& exit

    ECHO      Starting RhoConnect instance on port !rhoConnectPort!...
      REM Remove ' ^& exit' from end if debugging to display build errors
      REM The command window closes immediately after encountering them otherwise
      START /MIN CMD /E:ON /K %rubyCmd% ^
          ^& cd !projPath! ^
          ^& title !rhoConnectProject! ^
          ^& rackup -p !rhoConnectPort! -s thin config.ru --pid settings\RhoConnect.pid ^
          ^& exit
  )
  ECHO.
GOTO start

REM Load a Command Prompt window with Ruby, move to the applicable directory, and run the appropriate
commands
:startonlyrho
  CLS
  ECHO Attempting to start !rhoConnectProject! without REDIS...
  ECHO This will not work if REDIS is not already running...
  ECHO.
  ECHO      Starting !rhoConnectProject!...
    REM Removed ' ^& exit' from end for debugging to display build errors
    REM The command window closes immediately after encountering them otherwise
    START /MIN CMD /E:ON /K %rubyCmd% ^
        ^& cd !projPath! ^
        ^& title !rhoConnectProject! ^
        ^& rackup -p !rhoConnectPort! -s thin config.ru --pid settings\RhoConnect.pid

  ECHO.
  ECHO.
goto start

REM Load a Command Prompt window with Ruby, move to the applicable directory, and run the appropriate
commands
:stopserver
  cls
  ECHO Stopping: !rhoConnectProject!
  if NOT exist !projPath!\settings\RhoConnect.pid (
    ECHO      !rhoConnectProject! does not appear to be running.
  ) else (
    ECHO      Stopping the RhoConnect instance on port !rhoConnectPort!...
      REM Retrieve the PID from the RhoConnect.pid file
      set pid=DEFAULT
      FOR /F %%G in (!projPath!\settings\RhoConnect.pid) DO (
        set pid=%%G
      )
```

```
        REM Stop the instance
        START /MIN CMD /E:ON /K %rubyCmd% ^
                ^& cd !projPath! ^
                ^& taskkill /F /PID !pid! ^
                ^& exit

        REM Delete the RhoConnect.pid file
        DEL !projPath!\settings\RhoConnect.pid

    ECHO        Stopping Redis instance on port !redisPort!...
        START /MIN CMD /E:ON /K %rubyCmd% ^
                ^& cd %REDIS_HOME% ^
                ^& redis-cli -p !redisPort! shutdown ^
                ^& exit

    SET rhoConnectProject=Default
    set rhoConnectPort=Default
    set redisPort=Default
    set projPath=Default
  )

  ECHO.
GOTO start

REM Gets the ports to use for this instance
:prepports
  ECHO        Getting ports from ports.txt...
    if NOT exist !projPath!\settings\ports.txt (
      ECHO          The 'ports.txt' file was not found...
      ECHO            Creating 'ports.txt' file...
        (ECHO:RhoConnect:9292;)>>!projPath!\settings\ports.txt
        (ECHO:Redis:6379;)>>!projPath!\settings\ports.txt
      ECHO            Edit 'ports.txt' in settings folder to change ports
    )

  REM Get the ports to be used for the servers
  REM First, wipe out the existing ports
  set rhoConnectPort=Default
  set redisPort=Default

  REM Then, move to the correct directory
  cd !projPath!\settings

  REM Next, try to get the ports
  ECHO        Retrieving ports...
  FOR /F "tokens=1,2 delims=:;" %%G IN (ports.txt) DO (
    ECHO          Looking for %%G's port...
    set foundPort=0
    if "%%G"=="RhoConnect" (
      (set rhoConnectPort=%%H)
      (set foundPort=1)
    )
    if "%%G"=="Redis" (
      (set redisPort=%%H)
      (set foundPort=1)
    )
    if foundPort==0 (
      ECHO          Port name did not match
    ) else (
      ECHO            FOUND: %%H
    )
  )
```

```
GOTO :eof

REM Makes sure RhoConnect knows where to look for Redis
:preprhoconnect
  if NOT exist !projPath!\settings\settings.yml (
    ECHO     settings.yml file missing in settings directory^^!
  ) else (
    REM Update the settings file so Redis launches on the correct port
    ECHO     Updating the settings.yml file to be consistent...
      REM Delete any existing backups of settings.yml
      if exist !projPath!\settings\settings.yml.old del !projPath!\settings\settings.yml.old

    REM In reality, we need to rename it because you can't write and read a file
    REM at the same time.  Having a backup is good though.
    ECHO       Backing up current settings.yml file...
      RENAME !projPath!\settings\settings.yml settings.yml.old

    ECHO       Updating the ports in the settings.yml file...
      for /F "delims=" %%G in (!projPath!\settings\settings.yml.old) DO (
        set line=%%G
        if "!line:~0,9!"=="  :redis:" (set line=  :redis: localhost:!redisPort!)
        if "!line:~0,14!"=="  :syncserver:" (set line=  :syncserver:
%rhoConnectURL%:!rhoConnectPort!/api/application/)
        (ECHO:!line!)>>!projPath!\settings\settings.yml
      )
  )
GOTO :eof

REM Makes sure Redis has the correct port specified
:prepredis
  REM We need to a redis.conf file that contains all the settings (including
  REM the port) to launch Redis
  ECHO     Preparing Redis for the instance...
  if NOT exist !projPath!\settings\redis.conf (
    ECHO       Missing redis.conf file...
    ECHO         Copying default redis.conf file...
    copy %REDIS_HOME%\redis.conf !projPath!\settings\redis.conf
  ) else (
    REM Delete any existing backups of settings.yml
    if exist !projPath!\settings\redis.conf.old del !projPath!\settings\redis.conf.old
  )

  REM In reality, we need to rename it because you can't write and read a file
  REM at the same time.  Having a backup is good though.
  ECHO       Backing up current redis.conf file...
    RENAME !projPath!\settings\redis.conf redis.conf.old

  REM Make sure the port in the config file matches the one in the ports.txt file
  REM This is a slightly larger file, but checking it every time is the only way to
  REM be sure it is up to date.
  ECHO       Updating the ports in the redis.conf file...
    REM This prepends all lines with a line number to preserve blank lines.
    REM Then, it strips the line number before echoing the value.
    for /F "delims=" %%G in ('type !projPath!\settings\redis.conf.old ^| find /n /v ""') DO (
      set line=%%G
      set line=!line:*]=!
      if "!line:~0,4!"=="port" (set line=port !redisPort!)
      (ECHO:!line!)>>!projPath!\settings\redis.conf
    )

GOTO :eof
```

```
REM Load a Command Prompt window with Ruby, move to the applicable directory, and run the appropriate
commands
:openconsole
  cls
  ECHO Opening the RhoConnect admin console...
  ECHO If the browser page does not load, RhoConnect has not finished starting yet.
  ECHO Try refreshing the browser page if that is the case or check for errors.
    START /MIN CMD /E:ON /K %rubyCmd% ^
          ^& cd !projPath! ^
          ^& rhoconnect web ^
          ^& exit
  ECHO.
  ECHO.
GOTO start

REM Load a Command Prompt window with Ruby, move to the applicable directory
:openprompt
  cls
  ECHO Opening a Command Prompt with Ruby...
    if !rhoConnectProject!==Default (
      START CMD /E:ON /K %rubyCmd% ^
            ^& title !rhoConnectProject!
    ) else (
      START CMD /E:ON /K %rubyCmd% ^
            ^& cd !projPath! ^
            ^& title !rhoConnectProject!
    )
  ECHO.
  ECHO.
GOTO start
```

Create Server Services.bat

This file may also be downloaded from Oak Tree's RhoMobile Dropbox site.

```
@ECHO off
REM Type 'help color' in a command window to view color options
color 1B
title Server Services

REM Resource Kit installation path
SET resourceKit=C:\ResourceKit

REM Update the value with your Rhodes workspace path
REM Redis database dump is also stored in this directory
SET rhoAppPath=C:\RhoConnect

REM Update the path to your Ruby bin
SET rubyBin=C:\Ruby193\bin

setlocal EnableDelayedExpansion

REM Set some variables that get set based on user actions
SET rhoConnectProject=Default
set rhoConnectPort=Default
set redisPort=Default
set projPath=Default

REM Present options to the user
:start
  ECHO Choose an option:
  ECHO.
```

```
    ECHO   0 - Exit
    ECHO   1 - Install service for RhoConnect instance
    ECHO   2 - Uninstall service for RhoConnect instance
    ECHO.

  REM Prompt for a selection and handle it
  SET /p choice="Enter your choice: "
    if "%choice%"=="0" exit
    if "%choice%"=="1" GOTO installservice
    if "%choice%"=="2" GOTO uninstallservice
  ECHO Invalid choice: %choice%
  ECHO.
  PAUSE
  cls
GOTO start

REM SET Server that user is working with
:selectinstance
  cls

  REM First, count the instances
  SET total=0
  for /d %%X in (%rhoAppPath%\*) do SET /a total+=1

  if %total%==0 (
    ECHO No RhoConnect instances were found.
    ECHO Verify path in batch file and project locations.
    ECHO.
    GOTO start
  ) else (
    ECHO RhoConnect Instances:
    ECHO.

    REM List the available instances and present them for selection
    SET total=0
    for /d %%X in (%rhoAppPath%\*) do (
      SET /a total+=1
      SET instancePath=%%X
      SET instancePath=!instancePath:%rhoAppPath%\=!
      ECHO !total!. !instancePath!
    )
    ECHO.

    REM Have the user select an instance
    SET total=0
    SET /p instanceChoice="RhoConnect Instance: "
    SET instanceRequested="notrealfolder"

    for /d %%X in (%rhoAppPath%\*) do (
      SET /a total+=1
      if "!total!"=="!instanceChoice!" (
        SET instanceRequested=%%X
        REM Replace the Application Path with nothing so we just have the instance name
        SET instanceRequested=!instanceRequested:%rhoAppPath%\=!
      )
    )

    REM Locate the selection
    if exist %rhoAppPath%\!instanceRequested! (
      SET rhoConnectProject=!instanceRequested!
      SET projPath=%rhoAppPath%\!instanceRequested!
```

```
      ECHO.
      ECHO !instanceRequested!
      ECHO    Verifying configuration...

      REM Prep the instance if any files are missing
      CALL :prepports

    ) else (
      ECHO    RhoConnect instance not found.
      ECHO.
      GOTO start
    )

  )
  ECHO.
GOTO :eof

REM Create a service for the RhoConnect project
:installservice
  CALL :selectinstance

  ECHO Creating Services...
    REM See if service is already created by querying the registry
    REM Store result in temp file.
    SET basePath=HKLM\System\CurrentControlSet\Services
    REG QUERY "%basePath%\RhoConnect !rhoConnectProject!" /ve > %rhoAppPath%\temp.txt 2>&1
    SET queryResult=Default

    REM Read the result from the text file
    FOR /F "delims=" %%G  IN (%rhoAppPath%\temp.txt) DO (
      SET queryResult=%%G
    )

    if NOT "!queryResult:~0,5!"=="ERROR" (
      REM Service already installed
      ECHO    Service already installed.  Should be called:
      ECHO       RhoConnect: RhoConnect !rhoConnectProject!
      ECHO       Redis:      Redis !rhoConnectProject!

    ) else  (
      REM Service not installed
      REM Move to resource kit directory
      cd %resourceKit%
      ECHO %resourceKit%

      REM Add service for RhoConnect
      Instsrv "RhoConnect !rhoConnectProject!" "%resourceKit%\Srvany.exe"

      REM Add service for Redis
      Instsrv "Redis !rhoConnectProject!" "%resourceKit%\Srvany.exe"

      ECHO.
      ECHO    Service installed as:
      ECHO       RhoConnect: RhoConnect !rhoConnectProject!
      ECHO       Redis:      Redis !rhoConnectProject!

      REM Add parameters
      ECHO.
      ECHO    Updating registry parameters to run commands...

      ECHO       Processing Redis...
      ECHO          Adding Parameters key...
        REG ADD "%basePath%\Redis !rhoConnectProject!\Parameters" >nul
```

```
       ECHO       Adding Application value...
         REG ADD "%basePath%\Redis !rhoConnectProject!\Parameters" ^
             /v Application /t REG_SZ /d %REDIS_HOME%\redis-server.exe >nul
       ECHO       Adding AppDirectory value...
         REG ADD "%basePath%\Redis !rhoConnectProject!\Parameters" ^
             /v AppDirectory /t REG_SZ /d !projPath!\settings >nul
       ECHO       Adding AppParameters value...
         REG ADD "%basePath%\Redis !rhoConnectProject!\Parameters" ^
             /v AppParameters /t REG_SZ /d "redis.conf"
       ECHO       Adding service description...
         SC description "Redis !rhoConnectProject!" "Uses port !redisPort!.  In memory database used by
RhoConnect.  Must be running for RhoConnect to work."

       ECHO       Processing RhoConnect...
       ECHO       Adding Parameters key...
         REG ADD "%basePath%\RhoConnect !rhoConnectProject!\Parameters" >nul
       ECHO       Adding Application value...
         REG ADD "%basePath%\RhoConnect !rhoConnectProject!\Parameters" ^
             /v Application /t REG_SZ /d %rubyBin%\rackup.bat >nul
       ECHO       Adding AppDirectory value...
         REG ADD "%basePath%\RhoConnect !rhoConnectProject!\Parameters" ^
             /v AppDirectory /t REG_SZ /d !projPath! >nul
       ECHO       Adding AppParameters value...
         REG ADD "%basePath%\RhoConnect !rhoConnectProject!\Parameters" ^
             /v AppParameters /t REG_SZ ^
             /d "-p !rhoConnectPort! -s thin config.ru --pid settings\RhoConnect.pid"
       ECHO       Adding service description...
         SC description "RhoConnect !rhoConnectProject!" "Uses port !rhoConnectPort!.  Manages data
syncronization between mobile applications and data sources.  Requires Redis to work."
       ECHO       Adding dependency on Redis service...
         SC CONFIG "RhoConnect !rhoConnectProject!" depend= "Redis !rhoConnectProject!"
     )

    REM Clean up temp file
    ECHO.
    ECHO   Cleaning up...
    DEL %rhoAppPath%\temp.txt

  ECHO.
GOTO start

REM Remove an installed RhoConnect service
:uninstallservice
  CALL :selectinstance

  ECHO Removing services for !rhoConnectProject!...
    REM Move to resource kit directory
    cd %resourceKit%

    REM Stop the service if it is running... can't remove otherwise
    SC STOP "RhoConnect !rhoConnectProject!"
    REM Remove RhoConnect service
    INSTSRV "RhoConnect !rhoConnectProject!" REMOVE

    ECHO   RhoConnect !rhoConnectProject! service removed...

    REM Stop the service if it is running... can't remove otherwise
    SC STOP "Redis !rhoConnectProject!"
    REM Remove Redis service
    INSTSRV "Redis !rhoConnectProject!" REMOVE

    ECHO   Redis !rhoConnectProject! service removed...
```

|

```
  ECHO.
GOTO start

REM Gets the ports to use for this instance
:prepports
  ECHO      Getting ports from ports.txt...
    if NOT exist !projPath!\settings\ports.txt (
      ECHO        The 'ports.txt' file was not found...
      ECHO         Creating 'ports.txt' file...
        (ECHO:RhoConnect:9292;)>>!projPath!\settings\ports.txt
        (ECHO:Redis:6379;)>>!projPath!\settings\ports.txt
      ECHO          Edit 'ports.txt' in settings folder to change ports
    )

  REM Get the ports to be used for the servers
  REM First, wipe out the existing ports
  set rhoConnectPort=Default
  set redisPort=Default

  REM Then, move to the correct directory
  cd !projPath!\settings

  REM Next, try to get the ports
  ECHO        Retrieving ports...
  FOR /F "tokens=1,2 delims=:;" %%G IN (ports.txt) DO (
    ECHO         Looking for %%G's port...
    set foundPort=0
    if "%%G"=="RhoConnect" (
      (set rhoConnectPort=%%H)
      (set foundPort=1)
    )
    if "%%G"=="Redis" (
      (set redisPort=%%H)
      (set foundPort=1)
    )
    if foundPort==0 (
      ECHO          Port name did not match
    ) else (
      ECHO          FOUND: %%H
    )
  )
GOTO :eof
```